Snowflakes

IN SUMMER TIME

Dedicated
to the memory of my father

Frank Thomas McCall, Sr.

*Whose quiet influence lives on
in his children
and grandchildren.*

Jack McCall

A
Special Thanks
To:

Liz Ferrell
For her editorial skills and encouraging spirit

My assistant
Flo Agee
For keeping loose ends tied up and projects on time

My friend
William D. Mize
For his affirming words

Writer and friend
Johnnie Godwin
*Whose wisdom and patient counsel
started me on a writer's journey*

Contents

Chapter 1   The Welder 1

Chapter 2   The Boys of Summer 7

Chapter 3   Ol' Bethel 13

Chapter 4   Buster Brown Shoes 19

Chapter 5   Old Barns 27

Chapter 6   Throwing Rocks 31

Chapter 7   Sunday Dinner 39

Chapter 8   When Water Was Free 45

Chapter 9   Cold on the Mountain 51

Chapter 10 Defining Moments 57

Chapter 11 When Long Sideburns Were In 63

Chapter 12 Driving a Straight Shift 69

Chapter 13 Angels on our Shoulders 77

Chapter 14 Jingle Bells in June 83

Chapter 15 Tee Ball .91

Chapter 16 Gone Too Soon 99

Chapter 17 The Lost Log Chain 105

Chapter 18 Giving up the Car Keys 111

Chapter 19 The Power of Words 121

Chapter 20 The Long Goodbye 127

Introduction

Beyond the end of my driveway on northern bound Walnut Grove Road lies a hill of considerable elevation. I say considerable elevation because I have walked and/or jogged that hill hundreds of times. It will take the wind out of the most seasoned runner. The distance from top to bottom on both sides is no more than 200 yards.

On the opposite side of the hill the road flattens into a deceptive curve that rolls to the right. The outside of the curve is guarded by a giant poplar tree with towering limbs that lend their shade. The inside is crowded by thick woods. Gently sloping hills to the west provide a natural channel for funneling spring and fall rainwater and gentle breezes to this one particular spot in the road. A large culvert runs underneath and opens into a creek bed filled with deep, fine creek gravel. In this setting nature plays a deliciously surprising trick.

In the late afternoon and just after dark, in this curve between tree and woods, above cool creek gravel lies a pocket of cool air. It is fully ten degrees cooler than the air around it. There is no mistaking when you enter it and when you leave it. And it is almost always there. I've encountered it hundreds of times. It is beyond refreshing, it is exhilarating. The anticipation of knowing it will be there makes it even more so.

It seems that it snowed more when I was a boy. The snow was cleaner then. We made lots of snow cream. I especially enjoyed standing out in a snow storm. I would turn my face to the sky, open my mouth wide, stick out my tongue and try to catch snowflakes on it. Not very many landed on my tongue. But I did get a face full. They felt cool and refreshing even in the cold of winter.

I thought of those snowflakes the first times that I encountered that air pocket on Walnut Grove Road. The sense of refreshment was very similar. I contemplated how refreshing snowflakes might be in summer.

To feel refreshed is a tantalizing thought. And we all need to be refreshed from time to time, physically, mentally, emotionally, even spiritually.

We may find refreshment in the laughter of a child, in the sparkling eyes of a loving friend, in feeling love or being loved, in the satisfaction of a lesson learned, in a treasured gift, in laughter that resonates deep inside, in recalling a memory that is precious to us, or simply by counting our blessings.

I hope you find refreshment in the pages that follow. Sometimes it comes as a surprise like a cool pocket of air on a country road. Sometimes it comes in the form of a miracle......like Snowflakes in Summer Time. **JM**

1

The Welder

The Welder

GROWING UP, MY BROTHERS AND I LOVED to tag along with our father when he went to Carthage.

When he offered, "Come on, boys, we're going to town," we were ready to go. Going to town could mean a trip to the Co-op, a stop at the feed mill, or a visit to the tobacco warehouse or the stockyard. Sometimes he checked in on things at our grandfather McCall's furniture store. That was not our favorite stop. We had three uncles there who teased us unmercifully.

If we were lucky, he would stop at a local general store and give each of us a nickel to buy a ten ounce soft drink. We thought we were in hog heaven.

One spring morning our father returned from plowing in the river bottom and announced he had broken a piece on the turning plow. He would have to go to town to the welding shop and get it repaired before he could finish plowing. He asked if any of us would like to go with him. As I recall, he had three takers.

We all piled in the pickup and off we went. When we arrived at the welding shop, we followed our father inside.

The welder was a short man of medium build. He wore dark blue work clothes. The front of his shirt and pants were black with the grit of the welding shop. I noticed he wore heavy black steel-toed work boots with tan boot laces. Even though his boots were covered by his pants, I imagined they laced up almost to his knees. The welder had extended the life of his boots by keeping them well oiled. It made them black-black.

I also noticed, on the right side of one boot, that some stitches had begun to come loose where the leather formed a corner just below the bottom eyelet. It was especially noticeable because the corner had curled up, creating a hole through which you could see a small patch of the welder's bright white sock.

The welder secured the plow piece in place with two clamps and placed a new welding rod in the electrode. He gave his head a jerk of a nod and his welding mask fell over his face. The welding machine arced a familiar "Zzzzzzzht Zzzzzzzzzht" and he was about his business. A bright splash of sparks cascaded from the point of contact. The end of the welding rod burned from yellow to white to blue. As the weld began to "take," tiny molten balls of metal fell to the concrete floor and danced in all directions like spilled BB's.

The welder was halfway through his work when one of those little red-hot balls of metal jumped in the aforementioned hole in his boot.

With a sudden backward jerk of his head, he popped the welding mask back and started squalling, "Wooo wooo!" He grabbed the cuff of his pants and jerked his pants leg up over his knee. The boots were as tall as I had imagined. With the fingers of both hands he tore wildly at the boot laces as he hopped on his left foot, but his fingers could not work fast enough. He hopped faster. He made two complete 360's as he worked frantically to get the boot unlaced. Finally, the laces were open enough for him to grab the back of the boot just above the heel and push it off. He was wearing the brightest, whitest knee sock that I had ever seen. And on the right side of his foot, on a line

3

between his ankle and little toe, was a black hole about the size of a large green pea. He rolled off his sock to reveal a boney foot that had never seen the sun. With the nail of his index finger he picked the hot ball of metal out of the little crater that had burned into his foot, and he let out the most delicious moaning sigh of relief I believe I've ever heard.

At that moment he realized he had an audience. Pausing a fraction of a second, he decided to act as though we were not there. It was probably best that he did not try to make eye contact. We were all biting our lips and looking at the floor or looking away.

He sat down on the welding bench and pulled his sock back on, careful to line up the hole in his sock with the hole in his foot. He followed with his boot. Slowly and methodically he laced it up, pulling each lace tight at each eyelet and hook. Then he pulled his pant leg back down, and, as though talking to himself, said out loud, "Well, let's get this job finished."

With a quick nod of his head, the welding mask was back in place and he went back to welding. When his work was complete, he maintained a serious demeanor as he and my father made small talk and exchanged money.

Our little entourage remained solemn until we were inside the truck and both doors were shut. Then we all came unglued, laughing, everyone giving their take on the welder's dance. My father teased through his laughter, "He was hopping pretty fast, wasn't he, boys?" He was indeed.

I've often thought about that day and how the welder could have handled the situation differently. If only he could have laughed at himself.

If only he had turned to his onlookers and said,

"Boys, I sure had the hot foot, didn't I?" We could have all laughed with him instead of at him. Or he could have said, "Boys, have y'all ever smelled fried foot?" But that didn't happen. He missed the opportunity.

Sometimes we just take ourselves too seriously.

2

The
Boys
of
Summer

The Boys of Summer

I'M NOT SURE WHEN IN THE LAST CENTURY baseball players began to be called the boys of summer. Nor am I sure when the sport of baseball took on the title of "America's pastime." There was a time when baseball was considered to be pure Americana. It was thrown right in there with Mom, hot dogs, and apple pie.

Organized youth baseball did not make it to Carthage until the spring of 1963. I turned 12 that year, which made it my first and last year of Little League Baseball.

Before my brothers and I participated in organized baseball, we played backyard baseball. When we were boys our backyard seemed like a big place. When I survey that backyard today it looks incredibly small.

In those days I appointed myself as the one responsible for securing the new baseball for the coming season. In the winter, I would begin to save my money for the purchase.

Every spring the Western Auto Store would mail out its spring catalog.

The catalog, a small 8 1/2" – by – 5 1/2" publication, contained only a few pages.

But on one of those pages the "official league baseball" was marked down from the regular price of $1.29 to the rock-bottom, low price of 75 cents.

The much-anticipated catalog arrived in the mail one day and I made a beeline for Western Auto on the next day. Mr. Clyde White, the owner, always met me with a friendly greeting. I was cordial as well, but I had big business on my mind when I entered his store on that day. I walked straight to the back to check out the new baseballs. They were always located on a middle shelf. There were never more than six or eight of them, stacked neatly in square boxes. I was always relieved to see that they hadn't sold out. The way I had it figured, there must be a big demand for baseballs at these prices.

I opened one of the boxes and removed the baseball. Then I carefully removed the thin tissue-like paper in which it was wrapped. After giving it a close inspection, I carefully re-wrapped it in the paper and returned it to the box. I closed the box and headed to the cash register.

I counted out my coins, which included 2 cents for the sales tax. Mr. White and I closed the deal for 77 cents.

When I stepped outside the store and onto the sidewalk I felt like yelling out at the top of my lungs, "Play ball!"

That ball would be the ball that we played with for the remainder of the spring and summer. We had very few ball-games called off on account of rain. Most of our games were called off because of darkness or because we lost the ball.

The northern boundary of our baseball field was the garden fence. Any ball hit over the garden fence and inside first base was a home run.

The southern boundary was the back of our house. In all the years we played, we never broke out a window. If a ball was hit far enough to dead center field it usually ended up in the chicken house.

First base was placed just in front of the garden gate. Second base was located at the edge of the well house. The well house was a 6-feet by 6-feet block building, no more than three feet high with a flat, tin roof. It sat right smack in the middle of our baseball field, but it never seemed to get in the way. We just played around it. Third base was placed just at the bottom of the back steps of the house. The side of the building we called the front shop provided a backstop for home plate.

We used everything under the sun for bases, among them a piece of plank, flattened tin cans, rocks, even baseball gloves that weren't being used.

One night, a member of our cowherd, while passing through our yard, left a big cow pile in the exact spot where second base was supposed to be.

Being country boys, we played around it just like we did with the well house. A week or so later one of our cousins came to visit us. We naturally got a ballgame up.

While we were laying out the bases, our cousin suggested that we use the "dry" cow pile for second base. We went along with him, knowing that cow piles weren't always dry underneath. We were careful to stand on the edges when we made it to second base.

Late in the game our visitor hit the ball sharply to shallow center field.

He then tried to stretch a sure single into a double. It was going to be close. As he approached second base, he went into a full, feet-first slide. But he did not slide into second base - he slid through second base. When he stopped sliding he was a full body length past second. My brother John stepped in and easily tagged him out. When the runner stood up, he was shiny dark green on one side from his ankle to his eyebrow. He protested by saying he was on second base. My brother Tom, always the senior official, countered by saying, "No, second base is on *you*. You're out!"

Our garden was known for eating baseballs. Foul balls and home runs hit to right field constantly found their way into the garden. If the ball landed in the cultivated part of the garden, it was usually easy to find. The tall weeds growing around the edges of the garden and the fence rows, however, presented a real challenge to finding lost baseballs.

Sometimes darkness called off the search for a lost ball. That meant the ball would soak up the next morning's dew. It was not good for a leather baseball to get wet repeatedly, but it happened. By mid-summer the red stitches on our baseball would begin to disintegrate. We solved the problem temporarily by winding one strip of black cloth tape around the ball to cover the breaking stitches. As more stitches gave way, we applied more tape. Usually, by summer's end we had a black baseball that nearly doubled its original weight. It didn't slow the games down. We played on.

Our backyard baseball season ended with the coming of church revival and tobacco harvest. By the time the tobacco was cut, put in the barn and stripped, and the corn was in the crib, our beleaguered baseball, bat and gloves were safely put away for the winter.

But just after Christmas, I would start pulling my money together again.

On the first warm day of February, at the slightest hint of spring, I would start thinking about that Western Auto Store catalog.

I can still recall the feel of that new baseball and the smell of new leather.

"Play ball!"

3

Ol'
Bethel

Ol' Bethel

MY GRANDFATHER HEROD BRIM'S NICKNAME was
John Rueben. Most people in the Riddleton community
of Smith County called him Mr. Herod or John Rueben.
I called him Pa Rube.

I can only remember two dogs that he owned. One
dog's name was Skip.

Pa Rube called him Ol' Skip. Seems he put Ol' in
front of every animal's name that he owned. Even the
mules were called Ol' Kate and Ol' Lize.

Ol' Skip was a big dog. We figured that he was part
collie. His entire body was a deep creamy color, but his
head was palomino gold. He was good-natured and
friendly and never met a stranger. And he was a
groundhog assassin.

His groundhog kills were well orchestrated and
carried out in lethal fashion. He preferred to attack from
the rear. When he grabbed a groundhog by the back of its
neck, he would lean back on his hocks and go into a
dizzying counterclockwise spin. As he did so, he would
shake his prey with such fury that the outcome was never
in doubt. When he stopped spinning, it was all over. He
would then bring his prize and lay it at Pa Rube's feet. My
grandfather obliged by skinning the kill for Ol' Skip's
supper. Ol' Skip kept himself in groceries for about six
months out of the year.

In the late spring, Pa Rube took the sheep shears and

gave Ol' Skip his summer haircut. He always left a switch of hair on the end of Ol' Skip's tail and stopped shearing right behind his ears. Ol' Skip looked like a ridiculous little lion for most of the summer. And he left the groundhogs alone until fall. It seems that their sharp teeth and claws were just too much for Ol' Skip until his coat grew back.

The other dog I remember was Ol' Watch. He was a black German Shepherd. And he was bad news. He and Ol' Skip rarely fought, but when they did everyone went inside the house where it was safe. It was a hopeless venture to try and break up their fights. They never fought to the death, but they would wear wicked swollen battle scares for weeks.

Pa Rube's most famous dog was named Ol' Bethel. I never saw Ol' Bethel. He was long gone before I came along. Although I can't remember him, I do remember hearing about him. Seems he was somewhat of a legend in the Riddleton community because of a singular event.

Brim Hollow, where my grandfather spent most of his life, lay about two miles from downtown Riddleton. The road that leads there crosses a wooden bridge and winds through two creek beds. That two miles of road could take you a world away. Pa Rube took that road out to Riddleton just about every day.

After he was grown, Ol' Bethel developed a habit of following the truck to town.

Pa Rube did everything he knew to break Ol' Bethel of the habit. He locked him in the corn crib and he climbed out. He locked him in a stable and he dug out. He even gave Ol' Bethel to his father-in-law who lived on the other side of the county. His father-in-law sent the dog back because he would not stop following him to town, either.

Every day when Pa Rube arrived in Riddleton, he would look back and there was Ol' Bethel. When he left his truck, Ol' Bethel would crawl under it and sleep until time to return home.

Of course, Pa Rube discussed his dilemma with all his whittling buddies. Someone suggested "turpentining," a process by which turpentine is roughly applied with a dry corn cob to that area of tender skin located just at the base of a dog's tail. The cob would remove the first layer of skin and the turpentine would do its dirty work. It resulted in the dog thinking his backside was on fire. "Turpentined" dogs had been known to run for miles. Some never came back. Pa Rube was too fond of Ol' Bethel to do that.

He had heard that tying a Roman candle to a dog would break him from following. He mentioned it to his cronies. They thought it was a good idea. Someone said they could get one. Plans were laid out and they picked a date to teach Ol' Bethel a lesson.

On the appointed day, Ol' Bethel followed Pa Rube out of the hollow as usual. When the time was right all those involved called Ol' Bethel over to the center of the road. Ol' Bethel panted happily. He enjoyed all the new-found attention. A twine string was tied loosely around Ol' Bethel's body just behind his front legs. Another was tied in similar fashion just in front of his back legs. That served as a harness to suspend the Roman cannon underneath his body. The Roman candle was positioned so it would fire between Ol' Bethel's back legs.

Having everything in order, they turned Ol' Bethel around and pointed him down the road toward home.

Then someone lit the Roman candle.

When the first round fired, Ol' Bethel dropped to his belly and hugged the ground, his eyes flashing wildly because he could not figure out what was going on. The second fireball brought his rear end up off the ground, singeing the long hair between his legs and sending him running like a blue streak down the road. When the third volley fired, Ol' Bethel found a gear he didn't know he had. He flatted out like a speeding bullet.

The delegation back up the road was caught up in waves of laughter. Then events took an unexpected turn.

Instead of continuing on down the road toward home, Ol' Bethel took a hard right turn and ran in under the barn that sat near the side of the road. The barn, built into the side of a slope, had a wooden floor which created a crawlspace underneath. The floor was at least three feet off the ground on the side next to the road. The onlookers rushed down the road and arrived to peer under the barn.

What they saw was Ol' Bethel running in a tight circle as if he were chasing his tail. As he did, balls of fire were being hurled in all directions.

In a moment, someone showed up with an armload of burlap sacks. Half a dozen men frantically crawled under the barn to beat out the live sparks and small fires. Amid the frenzied effort to save the barn, Ol' Bethel slipped away unnoticed.

He would never be seen in Riddleton again. He would not be seen back in the hollow for two weeks. When he did let his presence be known, it was to slip back in under the cover of darkness to eat the food that had been left out for him.

It was months before he would let anyone touch him.

Eventually, he recovered enough to forgive the family and once again enjoy his status as beloved family pet.

Even so, for the rest of his days Ol' Bethel would go into a panic at a hint of thunder and lightning. And flames? At the mere lighting of a match, Ol' Bethel would roll up his lips to show his teeth and let out a low, menacing growl.

There are some experiences one never forgets.

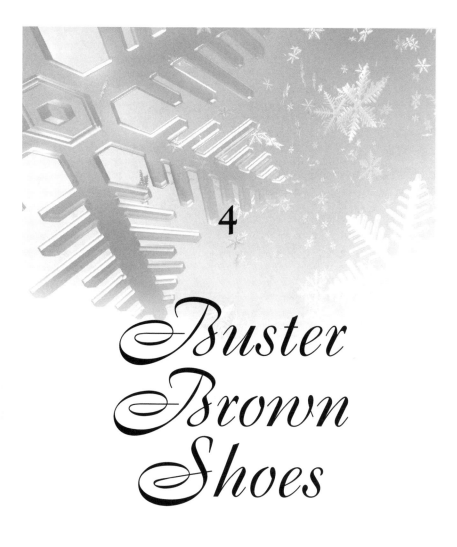

4

Buster Brown Shoes

Buster Brown Shoes

HAND-ME-DOWNS WERE A SUBSTANTIAL PART of our wardrobes when we were growing up. My brothers and I went through a ton of them.

We had a city cousin who was two years older than my older brother. That cousin was a steady pipeline for white sport coats. His mother was very kind to pass them along to us about every two years or so. When my older brother got the "new" one, he handed his down to me and so on. By the time our cousin was grown he had supplied all of us with at least one white sport coat. That is very important, because white sport coats were a must in the South on Easter Sunday. On that day you wore your very best. Thanks to our cousin, we looked the part.

We were taught to take care of our clothes because a little brother was coming along who would need them. By the time a shirt or pair of jeans or pants had made it through four boys they were pretty well threadbare. My mother always took great pride in saying, "The clothes you wear may not be the best, but they will be clean and slick ironed." And they always were. We wore those hand-me-downs with a deep sense of pride and gratitude.

Shoes were a different subject. Country boys tend to be hard on shoes. It was rare when a pair made it down to the next brother. My grandfather Brim said, "A man should always have good shoes, a good hat and a good suit of clothes." My mother saw to it that we wore good shoes.

I remember the day she bought my first new pair.

She drove all the way to Lebanon, Tennessee, to buy that pair of shoes. Twenty miles is a long trip to a little boy. I was five years old.

The store where we bought them was on the square in downtown Lebanon. I don't remember the name of the store, but I remember the name of the shoes — Buster Brown. My mother explained to me that Buster Brown shoes were the best money could buy. I can still see ol' Buster Brown on the sign in the store. Buster Brown wore a funny looking red cap and he had a dog named Tag. A round picture of Buster and Tag was sitting right down inside the heel of each shoe. The pair that my mother selected for me were high-top brogan dress shoes, rich chocolate brown in color with beautifully stitched non-scuff toes. When the salesman, with my mother's assistance, had determined the proper size, we put my old shoes in the new shoe box. That day I wore my new Buster Browns home.

As we turned off U.S. Highway 70 onto the gravel road that led to our farm, my mother turned to me and said, "Now Jack, whatever you do, do not wear your new shoes to the barn!"

The power of suggestion is a strange thing. Psychologists tell us that the part of our brain called the subconscience or superconscience does not recognize negative words. In other words, if you tell a child, "Don't run out in front of that car!" the conscious part of the brain hears that exact statement, "Don't run out in front of that car!" The superconscience, however, only processes the picture painted by the words....run out in front of the car. It's a pretty scary thought. It is far more effective to tell a child, "Be careful with your glass of milk" (see the picture), than to say, "Don't spill your milk again" (different picture). We are all inclined to fulfill the pictures painted by words.

I will go one step farther. How about this statement to a teenager? "Don't go out and do something stupid tonight." That picture has unlimited possibilities. On the other hand, how about trying this alternative? "Remember, be smart and be careful." Now that's a great picture.

When my mother said, "Now Jack, whatever you do, do not wear your new shoes to the barn," I could see myself approaching the feed barn in my Buster Browns. Besides that, my older brother Tom would be found at the barn and I, his little creep brother (my words, not his), wanted to show off my new shoes to him.

As soon as my mother was in the house and out of sight, I slipped off to the barn.

I would do well at this point to describe the entrance to the upper hallway of the feed barn to which I was headed. Extending a good twenty feet beyond the hallway at the barn's entrance was a god-forsaken stretch of no-mans-land that we shall call barnyard mire. In the wet season, which could last from early fall until late spring, it was a slimy bog to be avoided if at all possible. It was a nasty blend of soil and rain water and other foreign matter, both liquid and semi-liquid, usually associated with the bovine species. The muck could be from 12 to 18 inches deep depending on the most recent rainfall. It had a texture and consistency that would suck an overshoe right off your foot if you tried to run through it. At first glance, it looked black, but it was really dark, dark green in color. I knew not to go near it with my new shoes.

At the entrance to the hallway just on the edge of solid ground stood a gate which extended halfway across the opening. It was a make-shift gate that my father must have thrown together in a hurry. The planks were irregular in width and one of the two crossties was longer than the other.

My father had failed to brace the gate properly, and over time the planks shifted, making the gate look like the outline of the state of Tennessee.

The gate was even pointed eastward just like Tennessee. It was an odd-looking gate in an odd place. The standard, or crosstie, on the left side jutted a foot above the top plank of the gate. A loop of wire attached to the barn was usually dropped over that crosstie to keep the gate from being knocked over by livestock or blown over by the wind. Sometimes the gate stood alone, one end leaning precariously against the barn.

I approached the barn from the high side that day. The ground underneath my feet was firm and well drained. I carefully made my way over to the west barn wall. Then I stepped up on the edge of the barn's foundation rocks and, holding on to the side of the barn, I worked my way to the front corner. Staying on the foundation rocks, I edged toward the hallway entrance. When I got to the gate, I reached out with my right foot and stepped on the bottom plank. With no small effort, I shifted all my weight to that foot and swung away from the barn foundation. I worked my way out to the middle of the gate and climbed two planks higher.

At that very moment I saw my brother Tom coming down the hallway. I leaned back straightening my arms and crowed out, "Hey Tom, come here and see my new s-h-o-e-s!" I had not gotten the word "shoes" out of my mouth when I felt the gate moving toward me. In another half-second it was coming faster. I glanced to my left. The loop of wire was not to be seen. I was in a free fall. It was just the gate and me.

You've heard of a "belly buster" in swimming? That afternoon, I did a "back buster." If I had taken the fall on solid ground, it probably would have killed me. Fortunately, or unfortunately, I made a soft landing. But, in the middle of my falling I had managed to get my right foot free and my knee was bent when the gate crashed down on me. The force of the gate drove my knee between two of the gate planks, scraping the hide off my leg above and below my knee. Of course the impact knocked the breath out of me. For a moment or two I lay there, sinking under the weight of the fifty-pound gate.

Tom came quickly to my rescue, but it's hard to move a downed gate when you are trying to stay out of barnyard muck. He finally managed to pull the gate off me. When he did, I found I had two options. I could crawl out, or stand up and wade out. I struggled to get to my feet. As I stood up, I looked down. I could not see my new shoes, nor could I see the tops of my socks.

I must have been a pitiful sight as I trudged up the hill toward the house that day. My leg was bleeding as I limped along, and I was crying like I was dying. I was covered with barnyard almost up to my knees and so was my backside, from the heels of my shoes to the top of my head. Tom followed along behind me.

My father was sticking beans in the garden that fateful afternoon. He always used green canepoles off the river bank for that purpose. As Tom and I entered the back yard I was squalling at the top of my lungs.

Upon hearing the commotion, my father left his row of beans and started walking with purpose in our direction. I noticed that he had a long canepole in his hand. He must have sensed that something was amiss.

Instead of entering the yard through the garden gate, he elected to step over the garden fence at a low place. As he did, he broke that canepole in two over his knee. He left the big end at the garden fence.

Even though the fate of my new shoes was yet to be discovered, I knew I was in serious trouble. My father, obviously perturbed, gave us both a stern look and barked, "What's going on here?"

Desperate times call for desperate measures. I could see only one way out for myself. I lied.

Even though I was still crying, I managed to blurt out, "Tom pushed the barn gate over on me!"

Up until that moment, the look on Tom's face had been one of sympathetic amusement. Astonished disbelief is what I saw next. My accusation took him completely by surprise. He quickly countered, "Daddy, I didn't touch that barn gate."

My father grabbed my brother by his left arm and was in a full backswing with that cane when my mother appeared out of nowhere.

With eyes that could burn a hole right through you, she looked straight at me and demanded, "Have you got on your new shoes?"

My father stopped in the middle of his backswing.

I gathered myself and managed to squeeze out a whispered," Yes, ma'am."

My father let go of Tom's arm. Then, he turned to me

and slowly and deliberately, he asked, "Did he push that gate over on you?"

My goose was cooked!

Not only had I carried out an act of open disobedience, I had lied to cover it up. I could lie once. I could not lie twice.

I answered my father, "No, Sir."

He reached for my left arm and turned me around to have full access to my hindmost.

Did I mention I was wearing short britches that day?

My father whipped me with that keen, limber piece of cane from the tops of my new Buster Browns to the bottom of my short britches. To use a phrase from yesteryear, he wore me out. When he was finished, I looked down at the backs of my legs and they were dark green and white striped….for a few moments. Then whelps began to rise on the white stripes. That made my legs dark green and red striped. It was the whipping of my life. I deserved every bit of it.

I don't remember how I cleaned up those Buster Browns, but when I was finished, they looked like they had just come out of the box. And I must confess. Ever since that day, I have never worn new shoes to the barn again, not even once.

5

Old Barns

Old Barns

I LOVE OLD BARNS. IT SEEMS LIKE I always have.

My maternal grandfather had a combination tobacco barn and sheep barn. It smelled like sheep.

He fed the lamb in the barn's upper hallway. As a boy, I helped dock the lambs and weigh them on a hanging scale in that barn.

The main feed barn is where he kept his mules. It smelled like mules.

I can remember climbing up the ladder that led into the loft and sitting on a middle rung of the ladder. With boyish delight I would listen to the mules chase shelled corn around the bottom of their troughs with their lips and then crunch it with their big teeth.

On the farm where I grew up, activity centered around a big red feed barn.

That old barn is where I took part in my first corn cob battle. You have not taken a lick on the noggin until you have been hit with a wet corn cob. It would leave an imprint on the side of your head like a miniature waffle iron.

Most corn cob battles ended when someone got into a nest of rotten hen eggs. Aside from being sprayed by a skunk, nothing smells worse than being hit with a rotten egg.

I went on many an adventure in search of new egg nests among the bales of hay in that old barn. I learned to hold an egg up beside my ear and shake it gently. You could tell by sound and feel if it had gone bad or not.

My father tackled one of his least favorite chores in the hallways of that barn. At my mother's insistence, we seemed to always have a milk cow. When the cow came fresh in the spring, my father had six months of milking in front of him.

We never had a milk cow that didn't kick. They all played two devilish tricks on my father. One cow seemed to enjoy slapping him in the head with the wet, stinking switch of her tail. I've seen her jerk the hat right off his head.

My father was a good man, exemplary in his life and language. But one particular feat pulled off by the milk cows would send him to his limit. Sometimes the cow would kick at him and miss, then set her manure-laden hoof down in the almost full bucket of milk. He would grab a nearby tobacco stick and give her a sturdy whack across the ribs. Then he would holler, "You old _ _ _ _ _, you! The word was another name for a female dog. I think it was the closest to cussing that he ever came.

Some mornings my brothers and I would slip off to the barn and be waiting when he got there. We would hide in the loft just above the spot in the hallway where he tied the cow. Then we would wait, hoping the cow would do her dirty work again. Sometimes it happened, sometimes it didn't. When it did, we would roll on our backs and hold our hands over our mouths to keep from laughing out loud. It was high wire entertainment to hear our father trash talking to a cow. It was the HBO of our time.

My brothers and I have stacked more hay in that barn loft than we care to remember. It's where we hung tobacco on make-shift tier poles as we fought the sweltering heat and the yellow jackets.

On winter nights we filled the stables and hallways with our entire cowherd. We cut the strings on square bales of hay and filled the hayracks with blocks of hay. Agricultural research finally convinced my father that there was little advantage to bringing the cows inside at night. The troughs did manage to save the best part of the hay as the cows pulled it out of the hayracks.

And then, of course, there was the manure. Every two or three years my father would clean out the barn, one manure fork-load at a time. He would pitch it onto a flat bed wagon, haul it to the tobacco patches and unload it, one manure fork-load at a time. I must say, it made tobacco plants jump out of the ground.

That old barn….within its walls we pulled calves; dehorned cows with a hacksaw and a rope, and without a catching chute; and over the years, changed the attitude of many a young bull.

I love old barns. I think the reason is because of all the memories that are housed inside them. It makes me sad to see so many of them fall into disrepair.

6

Throwing Rocks

Throwing Rocks

THERE ARE MANY MISFORTUNES that can befall you when you grow up with a group of brothers and sisters.

When I was eleven years old, my brother John hit me in the mouth with the fire poker. That's not exactly the way it happened. Actually the poker and I did the hitting.

Here's how the situation unfolded. John was running through the house one night with the fire poker in his hand. I, his senior brother by four years, decided to exercise my authority and demanded that he put it back where he found it. He resisted. I, therefore, took it upon myself to right the situation by taking it away from him. We found ourselves facing each other with the poker in each of our hands, involved in a tug of war. He pulled, I pulled. He pulled, I pulled. Finally, I pulled the poker toward me with all of my strength and demanded, "Give it to me!" When I said that, he let go. The force of my pulling brought the poker up to my face like a steel trap snapping shut, and it hit me square in the mouth. Actually, it didn't hit me in the mouth. It didn't seem to hit anything. It was very strange. I put my fingers to my lips and found that I was not injured. Not until my tongue relaxed and found its place behind my front teeth did I realize that something was uncomfortably wrong. I ran to the bathroom and looked in the mirror. The corner, a good one third of my top left front tooth was gone. I cried. John cried. After all was said and done, "He didn't mean to."

In those days, a tooth could not be crowned until the nerve drew away from it. Dr. Robert Wright repaired the damage by placing a silver cap over it. I wore it for the remainder of my elementary schools days and all through my high school years. One of my nicknames during those years was Ol' Silver Tooth.

One Christmas, my brothers and I all got new BB guns from Santa Claus. We had a great time with those guns. We shot tins cans off the top of fence posts and broke more old discarded bottles and glass jars than I can count. We also made life uncomfortable for thousands of yard birds. But in all the years that we used our BB guns, I don't think anyone ever reported a kill.

One winter's day we were gathered out in the yard, each with his gun in his hand. We were discussing the pluses and minuses of each of our BB guns when my brother Tom , thinking that he was out of ammunition, took his BB gun and pushed the end of the barrel as far as he could up in the seat of my pants and pulled the trigger. He had miscalculated. It was still loaded. Never before nor since, have I experienced a burning on my buttocks like I did that day. Fortunately, the denim in the seat of my jeans was strong enough to keep the BB from penetrating. It did, however, create a bright red spot the size of a hackberry that, over the coming days, radiated out into a perfect circle the size of a fruit jar lid before it was finished. In the beginning it was black and blue, then it turned blue-green, then green-yellow, then finally yellow. I think I was the first member of our family to ever have a tattoo on my backside.

The most famous accident that happened to my brothers and me took place on a Saturday morning in a tobacco patch.

My father raised all the tobacco on my grandfather McCall's farm during the days when we were boys. One particular patch was located on the side of a gently sloping hill. The rows at the bottom of the hill were rather long, but as you started up the hill, the rows grew shorter. The patch literally covered the side of the hill. The west side of this particular tobacco patch was bounded by a hayfield. The rows ended on the east side at a dirt road that stretched from the top of the hill to a feed barn at the bottom. There were more than 100 rows in that tobacco patch.

We arrived there on a Saturday morning to "top" tobacco. Topping is the process by which the terminal bud at the top of the plant is removed by hand. This stimulated the plant to "spread off" by focusing its remaining growth in the top leaves.

Before we arrived to begin our work, feelings were already a bit raw. My brother Tom had made it known the night before that he would be leaving at lunchtime to spend the afternoon with his girlfriend pool-side at the Green Hills Country Club. Therefore, the day began under a cloud of dissension. As the morning wore on, the fact that Tom was leaving early seemed to be more and more of a subject of conversation. My brother John was particularly miffed. As the day grew hotter, tempers did as well. My father was not happy with the situation either, but he refused to get involved in the complaining. By the time 11 o'clock arrived John had worked himself into a frenzy. Finally, with some degree of relief and reluctance, Tom announced that it was time for him to leave. John was livid.

We were about halfway through the tobacco patch

headed toward the east end of the field when Tom left us and started walking toward the road. When he reached the end of the patch, he started up the hill. He was still within a stone's throw when John picked up a handful of rocks and began throwing in Tom's direction. It seemed like fun, so my brother Dewey and I joined in. Suddenly Tom found himself being peppered with rocks.

I was old enough to know that any rock larger than a marble could do some serious damage, so I was choosing my rocks carefully. Tom continued to head on up the road when two things happened at about the same time.

First, John picked up an unusually wicked looking rock. It was about the size of a small tangerine but it was rectangular in shape and had ugly sharp edges. He was eyeing that rock when Tom, for what reason I'll never know, rather than continuing up on the road to safety, decided to bolt back out into the rows of head-high tobacco. John calculated where Tom would be when the rock arrived, and launched it like a missile in the direction that Tom had headed. As the rock crashed through the top leaves of the tobacco, my father yelled out, "Cut that out! You're tearing up the tobacco!"

Then an eerie silence fell on the tobacco patch. It only lasted a second or two. The silence was broken by Tom squalling, "Daddy, come here! Daddy, come here quick!" With that he began to crash down across the rows of tobacco trying to find the row that we were in. Next, he cried out in a pitiful voice, "Daddy, come here! He's ruined my face!" He was crying now. It was the kind of crying that is a mixture of fear and rage. My dad started walking almost casually in his direction. As Tom approached us, he had his left hand covering his left eye.

At that moment, John started running in a westward direction crying, "I'm sorry! I'm sorry! I'm sorry!" When Tom arrived, my father reached up and pulled Tom's hand down from covering his eye. His eye socket was filled with bright red blood, now streaming down his face. Again he wimpered, "He's ruined my face!" My father stepped up and almost gruffly reached with his right hand and with his forefinger and thumb, he inspected the inch-long gash in Tom's eyebrow. He looked long enough to see that it was not a mortal wound and announced, "You're going to be alright." Tom was still crying and John was still crying — at a safe distance, of course.

Somehow someone managed to retrieve a clean white handkerchief, and my father mopped the blood from Tom's face. Then he took his red bandana and made a makeshift bandage and sent Tom on his way to the hospital emergency room. Before Tom left, John managed to get close enough to say through his sobs, "I'm sorry, Tom, I didn't mean to hit you."

Tom would go to see his girlfriend that day with three metal clamps in his eyebrow. I figured he would probably treat it as some kind of combat wound and make himself look like a hero in his girlfriend's eyes.

We stayed on and finished the job that afternoon and no one was very happy about it.

As far as I know, Tom never retaliated, because, after all, John really didn't mean to hit him. He was just throwing rocks.

Many other incidents and accidents happened to us as we were growing up. But in that setting, growing up with my brothers and my sister, we learned many things about ourselves. We learned how to give and how to take.

We learned how to forgive and be forgiven. We learned that every human being is a unique combination of strengths and weaknesses. We learned how to emphasize each other's strengths and down-play weaknesses. We learned how to love and to accept love. It was a great experience, but I will tell you this: that last ordeal stopped the rock throwing in the tobacco patch.

7

Sunday Dinner

Sunday Dinner

HAVING GROWN UP IN THE SOUTH, I HAVE, for most of my life, considered the mid-day meal to be dinner. When I was a boy and we were working on the farm and in the fields, we would stop work at about 11:30AM and "go to *dinner*." When we arrived back at the house, we would sit around the *dinner* table and my father would turn on the radio and listen to a program called "Noon Time Neighbors" on Clear Channel 650 WSM. After the opening song, a friendly voice would ring out, "From WSM, here's a friendly 'Hello' to all our noon time neighbors!" In the background you could hear a *dinner* bell ringing. Then, the voice of Tennessee agriculture himself, John McDonald would come on and conduct the show. My father was especially interested in the farm market report that was a part of every weekday broadcast.

I have no idea where everything got turned around. I suppose that somewhere along the way some sophisticated types decided that the noon meal should be called lunch and the evening meal dinner. I guess supper got thrown out with the dishwater.

Can you imagine Davy Crockett having lunch? Or, how about this? "All day singing, and lunch on the ground." It just doesn't sound right.

After church on Sunday, we had Sunday dinner. We had leftovers, if there was anything left, for supper.

There are three things that I distinctly remember

about Sunday dinner when I was a boy: fried chicken, mashed potatoes and Minnesota Valley green peas.

Since I am going to focus on the chicken in this story, I will dispense with the pea issue first. The only peas that ever graced my mother's dinner table came from Minnesota Valley. She would buy no other brand. As Forrest Gump would have said, "That's all I have to say 'bout that."

When you have mashed potatoes, gravy and Minnesota Valley peas on your plate, the possibilities are endless. You can hollow out a place in the top of a heap of mashed potatoes and go wild. You can fill the hollow with butter, gravy, peas or a combination of two or three. Or you can take one and stir it into your potatoes. We found it to be an unbeatable combination.

And, of course, we had fried chicken. Now when I say we had chicken, I really mean to say we had a chicken, as in one chicken. Which means the chicken was limited.

You couldn't just eat chicken if you wanted your appetite satisfied.

According to the way my mother cut up a chicken there were twelve pieces, not counting the liver and the neck; two legs, two thighs, two wings, three pieces of breast (which included the pulley bone) and three pieces of back, including the boney back. My mother ate the boney back because no one else wanted it. That left eleven pieces of chicken for six people. That meant two things. Somebody was not going to get two pieces of chicken and somebody else would only get one good piece.

So there was a lot of negotiating that went on over the chicken. Fortunately my father's favorite piece was a thigh. The youngest children usually went for the legs. We older boys spoke for different pieces from time to time. But it was always negotiated.

Everyone kept up with who ate which piece of chicken last time. My brother John could tell you who ate which piece of chicken on any given Sunday up to six months back. There was no cheatin' on the chicken at our dinner table.

The pulley bone was rarely taken in the first round. Usually two of us ended up splitting it. Of course, we were careful to remove the meat without breaking the bones.

At the end of every Sunday dinner we ceremoniously made our wishes and pulled the wishbone.

I have noticed since those days that the pulley bone has mysteriously disappeared from the fried chicken landscape. You rarely see a pulley bone anymore.

Shortly after Kathy and I were married, I was picking up a few groceries one day when I noticed a special on whole fryers in the grocery store. I think the price was twenty-nine cents per pound. I could not pass that up! When I arrived at home I laid the chicken out on the kitchen counter. Kathy took one look at that chicken and asked, "What is that?"

I said, "It's a frying chicken."

"What are you going to do with it?" she asked.

"I'm going to cut it up for you to cook," I said.

"Well, I'll cook it, but I'm not cutting one of those things up," she responded.

After that day I noticed that she only purchased cut up fryers with a label on the package that read "country cut."

I'm here to tell you that there was nothing country about those chickens. The pulley bone got lost completely.

And a country cut chicken only had eight pieces. That chicken would have never made the rounds in the house where I grew up.

Back then, if we had dinner guests, we still ate one chicken. That meant everyone in the family got bumped down the chicken line. Then, you were thankful just to get a piece of chicken.

If someone in our house had whined, "I just like white meat," they would have been asked to leave the table or been told to "take it or leave it." At our house, chicken was chicken.

I spoke with a woman not too long ago whose family chicken story was similar to mine. She said, "One day my oldest brother announced to the family that he was getting married and leaving home. First thing I thought was, 'Another piece of chicken!'"

I think the world would be a better place if more families had to share a chicken.

8

When
Water
Was
Free

When Water Was Free

THE BEST WATER I EVER TASTED came from the well
located in the corner of my grandparents' yard in Brim
Hollow. It was a hand-dug well that dropped over 100 feet
deep. When I was a boy I assisted in drawing many a
bucket of water out of that well. There were two buckets
involved in the operation.

One we called the water bucket. I still have that
bucket to this day. It's a white enamel coated bucket with
a red rim painted around the edge. My grandmother Lena
gave me the matching dishpan and washpan when she was
through with them.

That water bucket was a permanent fixture on the
back porch of the Brim house. It hung suspended about
five feet off the floor by a piece of #9 wire attached to the
ceiling. A hook at the end of the wire fit tightly around a
groove in the bucket's wooden handle. The water in that
bucket seemed to be the right temperature for drinking the
year round — not too cold, not too hot. Like the baby
bear's porridge, just right! Of course, we drank it out of a
dipper. I hardly ever remember drinking water out of a
glass when I visited Brim Hollow. When I became thirsty, I
headed to the back porch for a dipper full of water.

The other bucket we called the well bucket. I never
could figure out why it was called a bucket in the first
place. As a boy, I thought it looked more like a piece of
small galvanized stove pipe. It was a metal tube about four

feet long and about five inches in diameter, with a stiff piece of wire running from one end of the tube to the other on the inside. The wire was attached to some kind of trap at the bottom. At the top, it was turned into an eyelet about the size of a nickel. A strip of inch-wide metal was bent in the center and attached to opposite sides of the tube at the top, forming a triangle to which the well rope was tied.

That bucket was "let down" into the well by a rope that ran through a pulley overhead. Two posts on each side of the well pipe supported a cross beam to which the pulley was attached eight feet above the ground. The rope ran through the pulley and down to a hand-cranked windlass where it could be wound around like thread on a spool.

Hauling up two gallons of water from 100 feet down is no easy task, but I loved the whole process. Going to the well to draw a bucket of water was a special treat.

My grandmother taught me to let the bucket down slowly. We didn't want to "stir up" the well. The well bucket had a certain "feel" about it when it first made contact with the water in the well, like a fish gently tugging on a fishing line. Then we would listen for the gurgle. The well bucket made a bubbling sound when it was full. Then we'd haul it back up. It seemed that it took a very long time for the well bucket to make it back to the top.

When it finally did, we would raise the bucket then lower it into the bottom of the water bucket. I would reach and pull the "trigger" up at the top of the well bucket to release the water.

When the water began to crash into the bottom of

the water bucket it made a rushing, splashing, sizzling sound like no other I've ever heard. It's a refreshing, effervescent sound that would fade gently as the water bucket began to fill. The sound made me want a drink so badly I could hardly wait to wet the dipper. And the water, naturally cooled from deep within the earth, was always sweet and satisfying.

That kind of water will never be poured from a bottle. I think it's because the water yielded a satisfaction so closely tied to the effort involved in getting to it. It was the fruit of one's labor.

I have never tasted water like it since, nor do I ever expect to again.

Of course the whole water thing has evolved considerably since what seem to be those days of not so long ago.

When I was a kid, we thought we had struck it rich if we had a nickel to buy a "cold drink" aka "Coke" (in some Southern states a "dope" or "belly warsher"), or in un-Southern states, a "pop" or "soda." Whatever you called it, it was only a nickel. Today, we pay a dollar or more for a bottle of water and think nothing of it.

The best hotels supply bottled water in each room. A little sign attached to the bottle reads, "Please feel free to enjoy this refreshing bottle of water for only $5." So far I have managed to resist the temptation. There are two types of running water in most hotel rooms, hot and cold. Why do hotels offer a $5 bottle of water? Because someone will buy it! Go figure.

When I was a boy old enough to work, we carried drinking water to the fields in a gallon jug. It was one of those big-mouthed gallon jugs. Before we left the house we would fill it half full of ice cubes. These were real ice cubes from ice trays. They were as big as square golf balls. Then we filled the jug with tap water from the well. When the top was safely on the jug, we would wrap it in newspapers to keep it cold. Then we'd slip it down into a brown paper grocery sack and roll the top of the sack over the jug to keep the cold in and the heat out.

Upon arriving at the hay field or tobacco patch, we would set the jug in the shade until we needed it. By mid-morning it was time for a break. That water was so cold it would give you a headache if you drank it too fast.

We never took a glass or cup with us to the field. Everyone drank out of the water jug. Family, friends, neighbors and hired help all drank right out of the same jug. I was always careful to get my drink before the snuff dippers and tobacco chewers arrived. Sometimes if I was late getting to the water, I would notice an amber stain on the lip of the jug. I would either wipe it off with my shirt sleeve or move to the other side of the jug.

The introduction of the plastic milk jug changed all that. My father, ever the innovator, began filling used milk jugs half full of water and setting them in the deep freeze. When we started to the fields he would grab one out of the freezer and finish filling it with water. It was not necessary to insulate that jug of water or set it in the shade. It would take all day for the ice to melt. The water was head-splitting cold, too.

Sometimes we would run out of water toward the end of the day. If my brothers and I complained loudly enough, my father would challenge us by saying, "Go get a drink in the creek." We always protested.

He would walk us down to the edge of the creek

under discussion and say, "Now, see that little bluff right over there? A spring is running out from under there."

I will admit that a trickle of water flow could usually be seen. Our father knew exactly what he was talking about, but we never admitted it to him. Then he would say, "Just put your face down in the water right up next to where the water is coming out. It's as clean and safe as any water that you could ever drink."

That was easy for him to say. I always envisioned a snake or snapping turtle jumping out and latching on to my nose.

But, at one time or another, somewhere along the way, each of us became thirsty enough to try it. My father would watch in secret delight for this to happen. He would hold his tongue until we were down on our knees with our faces in the water just ready to draw in a drink. Then, he would laugh and say, "Be sure to clinch your teeth to strain out the bugs."

That was not funny!

9

Cold

On The

Mountain

Cold on the Mountain

WHEN MY GRANDFATHER HEROD BRIM DIED in the fall of 1963, my family "inherited" the tobacco allotment that came with his farm. In those days, in order to qualify for the government allotment, the tobacco had to be grown on the farm of origin. That meant we would be growing tobacco in Brim Hollow.

The best word for describing the Brim Hollow farm is "upland." In the past, a single field had been devoted to growing tobacco, but it needed a rest. Three small garden plots made up the other level ground. There was one other place called "the tater hill" where a garden had once been located in years gone by. I climbed that hill one time. To me, only big horn sheep and mountain goats would want to go there. It was no place for a tobacco patch.

In the head of Brim Hollow on the righthand side lay a twenty-acre field that many years before, was devoted to hillside corn. At the top of that field, just below a steep and rocky ridge, lay a long, narrow stretch of level ground about 30 tobacco rows wide and as long as two football fields. My father decided we would locate the tobacco patch there. As the years went by we came to refer to that tobacco patch as the mountain.

The mountain presented two special challenges. The first was getting to it, coupled with getting back down after you got there. It was a treacherous trip for a tractor. At harvest time we either brought the cut tobacco down with a mule and slide or took extraordinary precautions with a tractor and wagon. My father was never one to take chances with equipment. At two especially steep places he would lock the wagon tires on the back axle with a chain and drag the wagon down. That, he said, was to keep the loaded wagon from pushing the tractor off the hill.

The second challenge presented by the mountain was its soil. I've never worked in rockier ground. We jokingly called the rocks mountain gravel. They were everywhere, in abundance…..from pebbles to rocks the size of a grapefruit. When we found one as big as a man's head we toted it out of the tobacco patch.

That rocky soil grew what we called "frog-eyed" tobacco. It produced tobacco which had beautifully long golden leaves dotted with spots one or two shades lighter in color than the leaf. It did not weigh like we would have liked, but it commanded one of the highest government grades.

We never considered taking a tobacco setter on the mountain for two reasons. First, it would have been almost impossible to get it up there, and second, the ground was too rocky for it to operate properly. That meant the mountain had to be "pegged out" or transplanted by hand. And that could only be accomplished when the ground was wet.

On a disagreeable morning in the spring of 1964 we arrived at the Brim Hollow to peg tobacco on the mountain. As we started up the hollow, we were met by a misty rain.

I don't remember how we got the plants up there that day. I do know that we left our pickup truck about a quarter mile away down on the hollow road. Two days of steady rain had the ground well prepared for pegging tobacco. It was almost too muddy, even in rocky ground. As we stretched the string to mark off the first row, I gazed across the hollow. The clouds were very low and grey. The misty fog made it impossible to see from one ridge to the other.

My brothers John and Dewey dropped plants while my brother Tom, my father and I put them in the ground. As we finished the first row the mist turned into a light drizzle. Along with the drizzle came the slightest hint of a breeze. At first, we hardly realized the temperature was dropping.

We had completed three or four rows and were making good progress when the drizzle turned into light rain. The stiff breeze that accompanied it had a bit of a bite to it. The intensity of the rain was enough to begin to affect working conditions. After another hour we were soaked to the bone. We pegged on. But we didn't continue in silence. My three brothers and I began to lobby hard to call it quits. My father was determined to set out every plant that we had pulled that morning. We pegged on.

Then the light rain turned to a steady rain. By now the wind was howling. I say howling. Actually, my brothers and I were doing the howling. We were begging our father to bring an end to the madness. The wind was, in fact, whistling. The ridge provided a perfect funnel for a north wind and "she was coming 'round the mountain!" Even the ground was feeling cold to our bare feet. We didn't realize how cold we were.

My father was never one to get to the fields early. He ate his breakfast at 6:30 every morning and was usually on the job by 7:30 or 8:00am. But once he got there, he was

54

disinclined to leave until the job was finished or the day was spent. It appeared that he was not leaving that day until every plant was in the ground.

I cannot remember a time when I was so glad to see a bad situation get worse.

Finally the sky opened up and the rain poured down. I looked across the hollow to see the rain being blown in sheets. It was all over but the shoutin'. My father said, "Let's get out of here!" My brothers and I ran off and left him.

We took the route a crow would have flown, a diagonal line across the old corn field and through the woods. I think that red GMC Pickup truck was one of the most welcome sights I will ever see. Tom ran ahead, circled the truck, got in on the driver's side and fired up the engine. The four of us huddled near the center of the dash where warm air would soon be blowing. As we waited, I noticed that Dewey's teeth were chattering uncontrollably. Under the sound of his chattering teeth he was uttering an emotionless moaning sound. It sounded like an Indian death chant. I looked closer. His fair skin was pasty white. He looked like a dead man. I called his name in an alarming whisper, "Dewey!" He turned toward me with a lifeless stare. That's when I noticed his lips were dark blue.

That was the closest I ever came to seeing someone die of exposure in a tobacco patch.

10
Defining Moments

Defining Moments

I SUPPOSE WE ALL EXPERIENCE a handful of defining moments in our lives – those experiences and life lessons that have extraordinary impact on how our lives turn out. One came for me in late summer of my twelfth year.

My three brothers and I wore a slew of hand-me-downs. Except for socks and underwear, my mother bought very few clothes for us. When she did make clothing purchases most came through the Sears - Roebuck & Co. mail catalog. It was a big deal at our house when the Sears-Roebuck order came in the mail. Sometimes we watched for the mailman for days.

On an August evening I was working my way through the house saying my good nights when I saw my mother intent on a project at the kitchen table. I stopped at her side and asked, "Momma, what are you doing?"

"I'm ordering new school shoes for you and your brothers," she replied. That piqued my curiosity.

I pulled a chair up beside her and sat down, then half-stood as I leaned over her shoulder to get a closer look.

"Which one are you ordering?" I asked. She pointed to the picture of a shoe in the lower left corner of the right-hand page of the catalog. It was a simple, smart-looking black shoe with a smooth rounded top. Much like a military dress shoe, it had shoe stings laced through three eyelets on each side. I also noticed the price – 2 pairs for $5.

I allowed my eyes to scan the entire page. In that

moment, for the first time in my entire life, I fell hard, the victim to well-designed advertising.

At the top of the same page, in the right corner, I laid my eyes on the most beautiful pair of shoes I had ever seen. The shoe was sleek in its design, with detailed stitching around the ridge of the toe. And just above the shoe was an image of the planet Saturn. A space rocket was flying beside the planet. Lines of turbulence indicated that it had just encircled Saturn and was now headed back out into deep space. The caption beside the shoe read, "Designed with a pre-molded sole and heel made from a revolutionary synthetic material developed in space travel!" The price was $7.95.

I pointed to the top of the page and said, "That's the pair I want, right there."

My mother paused before she responded. Then, slowly and softly she said, "I can't afford to buy that pair of shoes for you." Her voice became firmer as she continued, "I can put shoes on three of you boys for what that pair costs."

I persisted, "But you don't understand, that's the pair that I want." Then I waxed brazen and I said, "And when I start to school, that pair of shoes is going to be on my feet." She should have slapped me silly.

But she didn't. Instead she took a slow, deep breath and in a voice devoid of any coldness she said softly, but firmly, "Son, when it gets to where what I buy is not good enough for you, you can get a job and buy your own."

That exchange began for me an exciting journey. I said, "Order that pair for me and I'll pay for them." On the first day of school, they were on my feet.

The fall of 1963 marked the opening of the first fast

food restaurant in Carthage, Tenn. Built by my uncle Dave Manning McCall and his childhood friend, Morris Myers, it was named for their wives, Rebecca and Glenda, respectively, and called the "G&R Dairy Chef" or "G&R." Years later it would change ownership. It operates to this very day as "Brenda's." Stop by if you are in Carthage. The food is excellent.

Anyone in Carthage with half a memory has a story about the G&R. Some still affectionately refer to it as the "Gag and Run."

In the fall the G&R opened I started my first job there at the handsome wage of 40 cents per hour. By working after school on two afternoons and on weekends, I could knock out 30 hours. After taxes I had around $11.50. Back then, that amount of money would go a long way. But that was not the best part. The best part was the meal allowance.

Employees were allowed 60 cents for lunch and 75 cents in the evenings. In those days fast food was still somewhat of a novelty. It was a bonanza! Oh, man, what 60 cents would buy! Hamburger – 25 cents, Fries -20 cents, Medium Coke -15 cents. And in the evening, 75 cents! Get this! – Cheeseburger – 35 cents, Onion Rings or Tater Tots – 25 cents, Medium Coke-15 cents, or add 4 cents and get a small shake.

That fall I worked my first 20 hours to replenish my savings after paying for that pair of shoes. It taught me to place a value on things that I bought.

I would buy all of my clothes for the last year of elementary school and throughout my high school days. Before I left the G& R, I was making 65 cents per hour – over $25 for a 40-hour week! And that was not bad. The best Farrar slacks could be purchased for $7 and you could buy the best short sleeved shirt all day long at Waggoner and Maggart Department Store for $2.98. When I was a sophomore in high school I bought my first three-piece wool suit at Waggoner and Maggart for $65. Eventually, I was furnishing my two younger brothers with hand-me-downs.

When I was a junior in high school I was offered the new position of clerking the livestock sale at Farmers Commission Company. It was there that I worked for one of the finest men that I have ever known, Bobby Woodard. The workday began at 7:00 a.m. on Saturday morning. The sale started promptly at 1:00 pm. The pay was $40 per day. Some Saturdays I worked eight hours and some Saturdays I worked 24 hours. I have a vivid memory of watching the sun come up through a small office window on Sunday morning on some of the larger fall sales. I worked hard, but I was paid well.

In the fall of 1970 I moved to Knoxville, Tenn. to attend the University of Tennessee. My first year there, I washed dishes and mopped the floor in the Agriculture Cafeteria. The position had its privileges. I was on a first name basis with all the power brokers in the college of agriculture because they handed me their lunch trays laden with dirty dishes every day. My final two years in Knoxville, I lived and worked on the University of Tennessee farm.

During my college years my father was gracious enough to allow me to keep a dozen mamma cows on his farm. The proceeds from the sale of their calves each year went a long way in getting me through college. When I finished my college days I had more money in the bank than when I started out.

In many ways I have lived a serendipitous life. But I have always appreciated what I've had. Someone once said if you have anything of value for which you did not sacrifice or pay a price, someone else did.

In all my years of growing up, I never once lost an article of clothing. It simply came down to this – if you paid for it, you place greater value on it.

Over the years, I have often thought back to that evening at the kitchen table and the conversation between my mother and me. I have come to admire her for her courage - the courage to deny me that which she could not afford. And I am increasingly thankful that she refused to pay for that pair of shoes.

11

When Long
Sideburns
Were In

When Long Sideburns Were IN

I've always been intrigued by fads. At least that's what we called them when I was growing up. Today we refer to it as style — you know, that which is in style or out of style. The kids today have a term they call stylin'. Of course, fads or styles come and go.

When I was in elementary school cuffs on blue jeans were in. If your jeans didn't have two- to four-inch cuffs, you were considered poor, or a square. By the time I reached high school cuffs were out and straight leg jeans were in. Solid color, oxford cloth shirts with button down collars were also in. And, of course, matching socks were a must. I had a sky blue oxford cloth shirt and sky blue socks, a burgundy shirt and burgundy socks, a forest green shirt and forest green socks, and yes, an Easter egg yellow shirt and yellow socks.

Most oxford cloth shirts of that day had a two inch strip of cloth sewn into the yoke in the back. It became a popular feat to remove those from the shirts of unsuspecting victims. The strip of cloth referred to by some as a "fruit loop" was removed thusly.

The perpetrator would sneak up behind the intended victim and upon yelling, "Fruit loop," would slip his index finger under the "loop" of cloth and give it a firm jerk. The strip of cloth was usually separated from the shirt quite cleanly. I did, however, see one of my friends get the back of his shirt ripped out because of a stubborn "fruit loop." I wondered how he explained that to his mama.

Some girls called the strips of cloth "love loops" and collected them from their boy friends. A guy would never have yelled "Love loop!" when ripping off a fruit loop. It would not have been cool. Cool was straight leg jeans, an oxford cloth shirt with matching socks and brown penny loafer shoes.

Thanks to the Beatles and the British music invasion, longer hair made a comeback in the 1960's. During my high school days sideburns made a comeback, too.

I think my first serious struggle with the sin of envy came about over the issue of sideburns. Mine were narrow and I could not grow them long with any consistency.

That was not the case with Billy Wayne Scruggs. Billy Wayne Scruggs grew the most bodacious sideburns of anyone in the class of 1969 at Smith County High School.

Well, Curtis Ellis grew great sideburns, too, but I didn't have to look at him in first period class every morning.

As I contemplated the issue of Billy Wayne Scruggs' sideburns, I came to the conclusion that he must have started shaving when he was 10 years old. His beard had a five o'clock shadow by fifth period (one o'clock) every afternoon, and his sideburns were long, dark and thick. He could have grown his sideburns down to his Adam's apple if he had taken a notion. But he chose to cut them off at the edge of his jaw and leave a point on them that reached halfway to his chin. The lead singer for the group called the Monkeys, Michael Nesmith, had sideburns like Billy Wayne Scruggs. They were really cool.

That's not to say that I didn't try to grow long sideburns. I did. But every time I made an attempt to grow them below the bottom of my ears, my right sideburn refused to cooperate. There was a spot in the front edge of that sideburn where whiskers would not grow. It was a square spot the exact size of one of those little pieces of unleavened bread that some churches serve at communion. I would let the sideburn grow longer then shave it off, hoping it would come back thicker and darker. It was not going to happen. My sideburns that didn't match became a nagging source of frustration.

One morning before school I was standing in front of the bathroom mirror agonizing over my sideburns. I must have looked in distress because it made my mother pause as she walked by the bathroom door. She gave me a quizzical look and asked, "What is wrong with you?"

I said, "Aw, it's this sideburn." I pointed to the one on the right side of my head and said, "Look, I can't get anything to grow right here in this spot."

She studied the situation for a few seconds. Then, her face brightened and she said, "Wait right there."

In a moment she returned with a tube of mascara. She withdrew the spiral brush from the tube and smiling mischievously, she said, "Bend over here."

I leaned over and turned the right side of my head so she could easily inspect the sideburn. She made two quick strokes with the brush so lightly that I hardly felt it. Then, she smiled broadly and said, "Take a look."

I could not believe it! I compared both sideburns....a perfect match!

My mother offered, "What you didn't know was there's some peach fuzz growing in that bare spot. It picked up the mascara pretty well."

Off to school I went, my self-esteem boosted significantly.

After that day, I would meet my mother in front of the bathroom mirror every morning to have my sideburn fixed before I left for school. A few weeks went by. Our sideburn secret was working to perfection.

Then one day it rained.

I don't mean it just rained. It poured. It was a hard-driving, frog-choking rain.

For some reason, I didn't even consider the fact that my sideburn was in imminent danger. I covered my head with my spiral notebook when I sprinted from the house out to the truck. I did the same when I got on the school bus.

On a normal day, the school bus driver would have circled the high school and let us off between the elementary school and the high school. When the weather was unusually bad, he would stop on College Street on the north side of the building and let the high school students off. A thirty-foot stretch of sidewalk lay between the bus and the side entrance to the high school building.

As I stepped off the bus that morning, a gusting west wind drove a sheet of rain that slapped the right side of my head like a wet boat paddle. In an instant, I was drenched. I raced for the door and stepped inside. After shaking off the rain water, I gathered myself and headed for class. As I passed the place where one of my buddies was always stationed by the trash can each morning, he called out, "Hey, your sideburn is running down the side of your face!"

I was mortified! I shaded the right side of my face with my hand as I made a mad dash for the boy's bathroom. I stepped in front of the mirror to take a look. It was true!

A line of black liquid was winding its way down the

side of my face and dripping off at the edge of my jaw. In a panic, I gathering up all the toilet paper that I could quickly unroll. Then I scrubbed the mascara off.

That night I raised my sideburns for good.

I saw Billy Wayne Scruggs at a class reunion a few years ago. He didn't even have sideburns. He had shaved them off above his ears. I guess they're out of style.

And me? I guess I overcompensated. I've had a full beard for over thirty years.

Well......it's not that full.

12

Driving a *Straight* *Shift*

Driving a Straight Shift

ALL MY FATHER'S CHILDREN LEARNED TO DRIVE on a manual transmission, or, as we referred to it, a straight shift. We were first introduced to a motorized vehicle by way of a Model A John Deere tractor. Equipped with a hand throttle and a hand clutch, it was easy to set in forward motion. Next, we stepped up to a Super A Farmall. It, too, had a hand throttle, but it came with a foot clutch. Still, it was not difficult to set in motion because the accelerator could be "set" before the clutch was engaged.

Things began to get more complicated as we graduated from a farm tractor to a passenger vehicle. My brothers and I cut our driving teeth in the hay fields on our farm on a 1958 GMC pickup truck, three-speed on the column.

There is an art to driving any vehicle that has a manual foot clutch. It involves a delicate balance of coordinating the engaging of the clutch and the manipulation of the accelerator — or as we would have said, "letting out on the clutch" and "giving it the gas." In theory it is rather simple, but in practice, not so simple. It takes a while to get the hang of it.

At first glance, there appear to be two possible undesirable outcomes if the engaging of the clutch and the accelerator are executed incorrectly. Too much clutch and too little gas and you kill the engine. Too much gas as the clutch becomes engaged and you take off like a blue streak. But with rookie drivers there can be, and very often is, a third outcome.

It happens when the driver gets caught between the right amount of clutch and the right amount of gas. It is as if the engine becomes confused. It gets caught between starting and stopping, and so the vehicle begins to buck like a bucking bronco. It can create quite an experience and even more of a sight.

I've seen my brothers dump half a load of hay off on top of my father's head as they bucked across the hayfield. To be honest, I've done it myself. If my father hadn't jumped off the back, he would have been buried under bales of hay. It was one the few times my father ever raised his voice. And did he ever then!?! Of course, that only made the driver more nervy.

To avoid such fiascos, we young drivers were inclined to "ride" the clutch. That involves leaving the clutch half engaged, neither "pushed in" or "let out." It made it less tiring on your leg. It also burned out clutches.

In later years, my father, with some degree of amusement, admitted that he had probably replaced at least one clutch for each of his children during our driver's training days in the hay fields. He just saw it as an investment in our growing up.

Of course, there is a third foot petal used in the driving process - the brake. Since drivers are equipped with only two feet, this can create another dilemma. Fortunately, there are few circumstances that require the driver to use the brake and the accelerator at the same time. In the hayfield there was rarely any need to use the brake at all. But the situation changes when a young driver takes to the highway.

When I was still in the learning process of mastering clutch and accelerator out on the public highways, there was nothing that put the fear of God into me like a hill, especially if I was going up that hill ….in traffic. If I had to come to a stop on a steep hill, I went into an absolute panic. There are so many things that can go wrong.

There I would be, stuck between two vehicles, one in front of me and one behind me.

My left foot would be pressing down on the clutch. My right foot would be holding the brake to keep my vehicle from rolling backward and hitting the one behind me. The moment of truth came when traffic began to move again.

Now I would need to move my right foot from the brake, knowing my vehicle would immediately start rolling backwards, and skillfully press the accelerator while simultaneously engaging the clutch with my left foot.

My greatest fear was rolling back too far and hitting the vehicle behind me, so I was inclined to overcompensate by giving it extra gas. That, of course, opened up another possibility - charging forward and tail-ending the vehicle in front of me. There was a scenario that was even worse: I could do neither and kill the engine. I have done just that more than once, I'm afraid. May God bless all those kind people who blew their horns to remind me that I had almost rolled back and hit them, or that I needed to re-start my engine and move on! I was just short of wetting my pants as it was.

With me and my vehicle still on the hill, the driver in front of me would be gone on his merry way while traffic behind me waited for me to crank my engine.

With my left foot on the clutch and my right foot on the brake, I would then rotate my hip so I could hold the brake petal with the toe of my right foot while pressing the accelerator with my right heel. The engine would roar to life. Now I had to take my toe off the brake and move it back to the accelerator. Oops - rolling backwards again! I was sweating! The driver behind me should have been!

I would press the accelerator as I engaged the clutch with my left foot. The engine would die again. I could feel the heat coming up behind my ears. I wanted to disappear. I couldn't. I would re-start the engine, doing the right toe and heel thing again. The engine would roar as I popped the clutch. Tires would squeal. My vehicle would jump three car lengths ahead, and I would experience an incredible sense of relief as I left the waiting traffic in my wake. The entire episode would unfold in a fraction of a minute but it seemed like half a day.

It took me a while to get comfortable with stopping on hills…in traffic.

I secured my driver's license in April 1967, shortly after I turned sixteen. In May of that same year I went out on my first date. It was the first time for me to drive to a young lady's house, pick her up and go out on the town. The event was the Spring Festival, a musical extravaganza put on by the high school each year. My date, two years my junior, had convinced her mother that it was not a big deal just to go across town, attend the festival and be back home by ten. Her mother sought the counsel of several of her friends before reluctantly entrusting her daughter to my care and driving.

When I arrived to pick up my date that evening, her mother reminded me to be very careful. I assured her that her daughter was in good hands. As we left her house, I had already eliminated any possibilities of finding myself caught in traffic on a hill. When I did take a street up the hill to the high school I made sure no one was following me. We made it to the Spring Festival just fine.

The program was enjoyable, but my thoughts were dominated by the excitement of being out on my first date. As we left the high school auditorium that evening we saw my date's mother and a female friend. We stopped to make small talk, and I offered to give them a ride home. To my surprise, they accepted. I was too young and too inexperienced to have thought the thing through. I had been driving legally solo for less than thirty days. At least I would not have to negotiate any hills.

We all climbed into my station wagon and started down College Street toward Main. I then turned onto Main Street and headed west. My date, her mother and friend were making animated conversation.

I was feeling pretty good about the evening. Then I made a glaring miscalculation.

As I attempted to turn right off Main Street onto Jefferson Avenue, I made my turn too tight. When I did, my right rear tire jumped up on the sidewalk and stayed up there for ten or fifteen feet. The sidewalk was higher where we came off. When the tire hit the pavement again, my passengers were jostled back and forth like the passengers on a Wild West stagecoach traveling at a high rate of speed over rough terrain.

We all laughed as if we were having a great time. I laughed the loudest in an attempt to cover up my embarrassment. My date's mother laughed too, but I noticed that it was a nervous laugh. In a few moments I delivered my date and her mother and friend safely to her door. They thanked me for driving them home and I sped away.

As I drove home that night I decided that the night had been a success. At least I had a good feeling about it.

And the young lady, my first date? I held a special fondness for her for quite some time after that night. I must note, however, that her mother never let her ride with me again.

13

Angels
On Our
Shoulders

Angels on our Shoulders

FOR MOST OF MY HIGH SCHOOLS DAYS I drove our family car when I was going out on a date. It was a white 1961 Chevrolet Parkwood station wagon. Appropriately and affectionately referred to as the "Snowgoose" by our family, it had a six-cylinder engine and a three-speed manual shift on the steering column. The Snowgoose was a "plain Jane" three-seater with the rear seat facing the back.

One Friday night during my junior year I was on my way to Hartsville to pick up my date. In those days the G&R Dairy Chef was a favorite gathering place in Carthage. As I approached the G&R that evening, I saw that a bunch of my buddies had parked their cars side by side in a row facing Highway 25. At the far end of the line of cars a classmate of mine was sitting in his recently acquired 1966 Pontiac GTO. It was candy apple red in color, and that night he had it waxed to a dazzling shine.

I pulled the Snowgoose in beside his car in the opposite direction to which he was parked. We were window to window. He smiled a big, beaming smile and asked, "What are you doing tonight?" I told him that I had a date with a Hartsville girl.

The next words out of his mouth were these, "Do you want to swap cars for the night?" I thought he was kidding. "Why would you want to do that?" I asked.

"Well," he explained, "I don't have a date tonight and I thought it would be fun for two or three of us guys

to back your station in at the drive-in and sit in the back
seat and watch the movie."

"Are you sure?" I quizzed.

"Of course I'm sure," he insisted. "Here," he smiled as
he pitched me the keys.

He got out of his car and as he walked away he said,
"I'll see you back here a little before midnight."

I parked the Snowgoose in a safe place and left the
keys in the ignition.

It's hard to describe how I felt when I opened the
door on that GTO. It was a beautiful machine. As I slid
into the white bucket seat, I was impressed by the high
oversized chrome console that supported the automatic
floor shifter. I also observed the white pillow cushion
resting on the console between the seats.

I placed the key in the ignition and fired her up. The
engine rumbled to life and played a music that only the
power cars of that era could play. I sighed a deep sigh of
satisfaction, shifted into drive and turned toward Hartsville.

When I reached my date's house, I turned in the
driveway, shut off the engine and walked to her front door.
I rang the doorbell and waited. In a moment she appeared.
As we stepped away from the front door, she noticed the
GTO. We made small talk about it as I walked her to the
car. I followed her to the passenger side and opened her
door. She smiled the cutest smile, acknowledging my act of
gallantry as she slid into her seat.

As I stepped quickly around the back of the car, I
could not help but think, "I have money in my pocket, a
date with one of Hartsville's cutest girls, and I'm driving a
Pontiac GTO."

There are a few moments in your life when you feel

like you have the world by the tail.

I opened my door and slid behind the wheel. As I did, I saw that my date knew exactly what that pillow cushion was for and was seated appropriately. She was a petite little thing, but when I turned in her direction, I was looking dead-level into her blue eyes. It took my best efforts to act cool.

I turned the key......music, again. Three hundred and thirty-five horses were at my command.

My date and I went to the drive-in movie that evening. I remember seeing my buddy and his friends sitting in the back of the Snowgoose and watching the show. He seemed as happy with our deal as I was. At the end of the movie my date and I headed back to Hartsville. We did cruise town a few times before I took her home. When we arrived back at her house, I walked her to the door where we said our goodnights. As I walked back to the car I had that lighthearted feeling that one always has when a date goes well. I looked at my watch....11:30. I had plenty of time to make it home by midnight curfew. I backed out of the driveway and onto the street. In a few moments, I was headed out of Hartsville. I was careful to observe the speed limit as I left the city limits.

I cruised past Big Goose Creek, by the three-way intersect of Highways 10 and 25, then over the first of the two hills that stand between Hartsville and Dixon Springs. When I crossed the second and higher of the two hills, I was struck by the brightness of the moonlit night. The sky was incredibly clear and filled with stars. It gave the night an eerie feel of daylight. The long, straight stretch of highway that led into Dixon Springs lay sprawled out before me like a silvery satin ribbon.

The temptation was just too much. Suddenly, a thought popped into my head. It came in the form of this question, "I wonder how fast this car will go?" I answered my own question by pressing the accelerator all the way to the floor.

When I did, every one of the 335 horses stabled under the hood of that GTO showed up at once. I had never experienced an automobile leaping forward. That Pontiac almost jumped out from under me. In a few seconds I was accelerating faster than I ever had in my life. Down the long stretch of road man and machine roared, 65 miles per hour, 70, 75, 80, 85, 90. As I approached the first of the two bridges that led into Dixon Springs, the speedometer read 120. That is when I experienced a car "floating" for the first time. It made my breath seem short and my head feel light. It's the feeling you get whenever you cross into forbidden territory. By the time I was approaching the second bridge, I don't know how fast the car was going. That's when I had a second thought.

This thought came in the form of a statement and it had a note of urgency about it.

It was shaped with these words, "You don't know how good the tires are on this car."

That was true. I rotated my knee to the right and lifted my foot off the accelerator, pulling my knee almost up to my chin in an exaggerated fashion.

The powerful engine relaxed and the car began to decelerate… 125, 120, 115, 110. When I blew through Dixon Springs and past Fat Taylor's store I was sitting on a flat 100 mph. Fortunately, I slowed faster as I headed up the hill and out of Dixon Springs. As I did, I looked up to my right. I could see the tops of gravestones in Dixon

Springs Cemetery glistening in the moon light. I looked down at the speedometer. It read 75. That's when the right rear tire blew out.

I used all of the next quarter mile and both lanes of the highway including both shoulders of the road to try to keep the powerful Pontiac under control. Believe me, I know what the expression "being all over the highway" means. The tires squalled and moaned as I furiously fought the steering wheel.

When I finally brought the car safely to a stop, I was on the right shoulder of the road in front of Mrs. Cassie Allen Griggs' house. I leaned back against the seat and held the steering wheel firmly on both sides to stop my hands from shaking. For a minute or two I allowed myself to relive the past few fleeting moments — moments in which I had come breathlessly close to the indescribable. I closed my eyes and whispered a prayer of thanks.

Angels on our shoulders. Do I believe in angels, you might ask? Absolutely.

I know of one who showed up in the nick of time to guard and guide the life of a foolish boy.

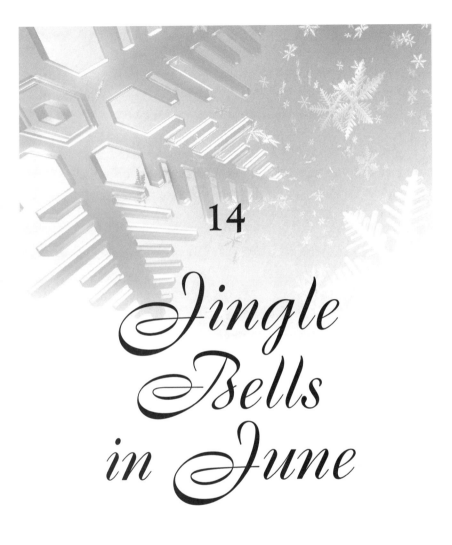

14

Jingle Bells in June

Jingle Bells in June

SAN ANTONIO IS ONE OF my favorite cities. It is a great place for a weekend getaway. In San Antonio, the River Walk is scenic and relaxing, and that great Tennessean Davy Crockett is revered as a god. And then there's The Alamo.

The Alamo is easy to find in San Antonio. It's right downtown west of the River Walk.

I was speaking for a professional group in San Antonio a few summers ago. The program called for me to make the same speaking presentation on back-to-back afternoons. I arrived the afternoon before and checked into the Adams Mark Hotel. I would have two unhurried mornings and two leisurely evenings to spend in a great southwestern city.

On the first morning I got out early and got in a two-mile jog. It took me by the impressive memorial to Crockett, Bowie, Travis, and Bonham, heroes of The Alamo. I circled The Alamo a time or two. As I did, I stopped frequently to meditate on its heroes and its rich history.

I returned to my room and reviewed my notes for the afternoon speech. Then I showered, put on comfortable clothes and headed downstairs for a relaxing breakfast.

The temperature outside was on its way up to 98 degrees. It was June 28.

The restaurant in the Adams Mark Hotel in San Antonio is an expansive lobby restaurant. It offers a full buffet, and friendly cooks are eagerly waiting to custom design   sumptuous omelets and waffles for their guests. I decided to have a plain Belgium waffle.

My cook was a big, friendly man of Spanish descent named Jimmy. He offered great service with a beaming smile. The morning had all the makings of a great one.

I returned to my table and sized up my waffle. After smearing real butter all over it, I made ribbons of warm maple syrup over it from side to side. Then I waited for the butter and syrup to slowly disappear into my prize.

Then the strangest thing happened. I was a bit shocked to catch myself humming, "We Wish You a Merry Christmas." I took note that it was the 28th day of June and hot as blazes outside. For the slightest moment, I jokingly thought I might be losing my marbles. I dismissed the thought and the song and returned to my waffle.

Then I heard it. On the opposite side of the restaurant, a little boy with an angelic voice was singing "Jingle Bells." I stood up to get a better look. He was playing with a small car, one of the "Hot Wheels" variety, and as he worked two sides of the square table, he was lost in his song.

The opportunity was just too good to pass up. I slid my hand into my pocket hoping to find a five dollar bill. I found a ten.

I walked quickly over to cashier and asked for the newest five dollar bill that she had. She looked in the cash drawer, smiled and said," I have two just like new."

I said, "I'll take both." I gave her the ten, thanked her, and paused to listen. The little boy was still singing.

I strolled over to the other side of the restaurant and approached the table where my little friend was playing and singing. I paused and turned to the woman who was sitting at his table. "May I speak with this young man for a moment?" I asked. "Why, certainly," she replied in a pleasant voice.

I dropped to one knee as I turned to the little singer and extended my hand.

"Hi," I said. "My name is Jack. What's your name?"

We were in Texas. I had made the assumption that he was a Southern boy. He was not. He straightened himself as if he were about to make a formal speech. Then, very properly, he pronounced his name: "Peter." He had emphasized each syllable.

I said, "Hello, Peter. I've got to tell you something. You sing 'Jingle Bells' as well as I have ever heard it sung, especially this time of year."

The woman was quick to his aid. "What do we say?" she snapped smartly.

He straightened himself again and said "Thank you very much." The woman smiled approvingly.

I said, "I want to tell you something else, Peter. It is okay to sing your favorite Christmas songs any time you want to. And I hope you always will."

Peter began to loosen up a little. His smile was more relaxed as he softly said, "Thank you very much."

"I turned to his companion and asked, "May I give Peter a gift?"

"Certainly," she replied.

I handed him the five dollar bill and said, "This is for singing so well. I will never forget you, Peter."

He said it again, "Thank you very much."

I turned to the woman and then back to Peter, "Is this your mother?" I asked.

His voice took on a serious tone as he replied, "No, she's my grandmother."

I turned back to his grandmother. She was smiling like he had just eaten a whole banana sideways.

I said, "You have a very fine grandson."

"We are very proud of Peter," she responded.

I turned back to Peter and said, "See ya."

"See ya," he beamed.

When I got back to my waffle, it was cold, but I didn't really care. I was still thinking about Peter. Strangely, I began to feel a little melancholy. I knew Peter would not be singing his Christmas songs very much longer. Soon he would grow up. Some little friend would tell him that he was weird for singing Christmas songs in June and he would feel self-conscience. Or maybe some well-intending adult would tell him that Christmas songs are only to be sung during the holidays. Peter would soon have to leave his innocence behind. I thought to myself that growing up is not all it's cracked up to be.

As I sat there lost in my thoughts, I had the strange sensation that someone was very near me. I turned to my right and Peter was standing so close he was almost touching me. He leaned against me and out of the corner of his mouth he whispered softly as if he were sharing a secret, "Thank you very much."

And then, he skipped away.

I have often thought of Peter since that day. I think I shall never forget him.

And he will probably not forget me. Because nobody else will ever give him five dollars for singing "Jingle Bells!"

He somehow reaffirmed my belief that we all should make the effort to remain young at heart. That is no small task, you know. I have known so many people who grew old before their time.

I was speaking before a group of savings and loan examiners in Kansas City not too long ago. As a general rule audiences made up of accountants and auditors can be tough. It has something to do with analytical minds, I think.

Somewhere in the middle of the presentation I found myself about three sentences deep into what I call the "Peter" story. I had not planned to use that story with this particular group. It's a little too warm and fuzzy for the analytical types, I had thought when I was putting the presentation together. But sometimes a story will drop into your head right smack in the middle of a speech and before you've had time to think about it, you're telling the story. And once you start a story, you have to go with it. To stop and say, "Oh, I don't think I'll tell this story right now," ….well, you just don't. For one thing it would mess up your timing. And your audience would be left wondering, "Why didn't he tell it?"

So, I was in the middle of a story that I did not mean to tell and while I was telling it, I was asking myself why. I've learned that a number of conversations can be going on in your head while you are making a speech.

At the end of the presentation, one particular gentleman sought me out. His hair was cut short military style and he worn wire-rimmed glasses. Everything about him, even his clothes, spoke of preciseness. In a voice almost void of expression, he said,

"I really enjoyed your speech. It was great, especially the part about the little boy and 'Jingle Bells.'" Then with a note of resignation in his voice, he continued, "And you are right. Life will beat that right out of him."

I suddenly broke into my best Bill Cosby impersonation, the one in which he is doing a Jello pudding commercial and acting like a little kid. With my eyes flaring wide and with all the little boy my face could express, I exclaimed, "But it's not going to happen to us, is it!?!?"

And in that instant he completely forgot himself and mimicked me as he said,

"N-o-o-o-o, it's not!!!!!!"

For just a moment we were both little boys again. And it felt good!

It's important that you keep the child inside of you alive and never lose your sense of wonder. Those who remain young at heart bring an enthusiasm and zest to life that is, in short, priceless.

15

Tee Ball

Tee Ball

WHEN OUR THREE BOYS WERE GROWING UP, we did the whole athletics thing- tee ball, Little League, Babe Ruth League, high school basketball, football, and baseball.

Our oldest, J. Brim, was known for his quickness on the basketball court and for his speed on the base paths. We shared in close wins and heartbreaking losses along with many memorable road trips.

Our second son, Jonathan, loved physical contact. He played center and defensive end for the 1999 1A State Champion Trousdale County Yellow Jackets. His high school football days were filled with drama and intrigue. He made his mark in Trousdale County Football lore.

Our third son, Joseph, inherited my father Frank McCall, Sr.'s mechanical genius. Along with that, he inherited my father's athletic ability or lack thereof. Joseph turned out not to be an athlete.

In junior high, he tried his hand at basketball. He finished that short career having scored a total of three points. His lone field goal was scored on the baseline, five feet from the basket. As the other team took the ball out of bounds, the referee turned to Joseph and said, "nice stroke." It would be the pinnacle of his basketball experience.

But long before junior high we had some indication that Joseph might not be a natural athlete.

Joseph retired from organized baseball after two short

years of tee ball.

His second and final year of tee ball found him on a great tee ball team.

The team was made up of good kids who were fun to watch and fun to be around. They won game after game and kept winning. The spring and early summer flew by. By season's end their record was 13-1. There was only one hitch. Another team in the league had the identical record of 13-1. They had only been beaten by each other. A playoff was scheduled to determine the league champion.

The reputation of these two tee ball teams had spread far and wide.

On a Saturday afternoon an overflow crowd gathered to see these two great teams square off. No one was prepared for the game they were about to witness.

At the end of the first inning the score was tied 5-5. When the second inning came to an end, they were tied 11-11. At the conclusion of inning number three, they were still deadlocked 15-15. The opposing team came to bat in the fourth and final inning and scored six runs. The scoreboard read 21-15. Our team faced an almost insurmountable lead.

Our first two batters made it on base safely. Suddenly, we were in the middle of a rally. Runs were scored, an out was recorded. More runners made it on base safely, more runs were scored, another out made. Our time at bat flew by. I checked the scoreboard. It read 21-20, 2 outs. We had runners safely on 1st and 2nd bases.

Our next batter was a little girl. She was so skinny she appeared tall for her age. I would say she would have weighed 42 pounds soaking wet. Standing at the tee she looked like a little pipe cleaner.

Because she was the last to bat in our regular line-up, I had paid particularly close attention to her during the regular season. She usually made an out when her time came to bat, but her outs were memorable.

She approached her opportunity to hit the ball as if it were some kind of irksome task. She always wore a serious expression on her face as she carried her bat up to the tee box in her arms as if it were a stick of heavy fire wood. After the coach had helped her set her feet properly, she would hold the handle of the bat with both hands as the barrel of the bat rested on the ground.

When she was ready, a scowl would come across her face. Then, with no small effort, she would lift the barrel of the bat up off the ground in hopes it would hit the ball on the way up. She never hit the ball very hard if she hit it at all. She was an almost certain out.

On this day she went through her regular routine. With resigned determination, she lifted her bat skyward. As she did her bat "dusted" the ball on the way up. The ball dropped off the tee and rolled lazily toward the pitcher's circle.

The little boy who defended that part of the infield was off the pitcher's mound in a flash and pounced on the ball like a bird on a June bug. He turned toward first base to through her out.

As he raised his arm to throw the ball, the unthinkable happened. The ball rolled off the tips of his fingers and fell to the ground behind him. He turned quickly in total disbelief, retrieved the ball and turned to throw it a second time. It happened again. He was astounded. He ran to pick it up.

On his third attempt, to his utter dismay, he did it

again! He rolled his eyes skyward and almost did a mocking collapse in frustration.

His comedy of errors had only taken a few seconds. It reminded me of one of the old silent films. Everything he had done was in fast forward and it all went wrong. It would have been funny but, at that moment, the stakes were too high.

I turned my attention to our little base runner. She was little and she was skinny, but she was fast; and now, she's on first. The bases are loaded, two outs. The score is still 21-20.

At this point in the game the situation had become so tense that grown men had climbed the chain linked fence, locked their fingers in the wire, and were swinging back and forth like caged orangutans. There were men sitting in the stands with the color drained from their faces because their wives fingernails had clawed into their arms. I was so caught up in the drama that I had temporarily lost our son and his place in the batting line-up. The crowd was going crazy.

I looked toward the on deck circle hoping not to see what I was about to see.

It shall forever be emblazoned in my mind, a big, red #10 sitting squarely between two narrow shoulder blades on the back of a mustard yellow tee shirt. Our baby was dragging his bat up to the tee box.

I've never experienced a heart attack. I think I have been close.

For a moment, I thought that I was going to die. As my heart leapt into my throat, I felt a sudden tightening in my chest. I could not swallow. I needed oxygen. I scanned the crowd for the EMS.

It had come down to this. With one swing of his bat, our son was going to be great or he was going to be a goat. The outcome of the game had fallen squarely on his shoulders.

Relief for me was not soon in coming.

He took his place in the tee box, then he started his practice swings. On any other day he would have taken two. That day he took all of four.

Slowly and deliberately he took the bat back in a mock swing. Then he slowly followed through with his swing, almost touching the ball. He repeated the sequence, three times.

At the end of his fourth practice swing, he did not hesitate. His backswing was crisp. His swing was so sharp that it reminded me of a steel trap snapping shut. The ball jumped off the bat into a low line drive.

The third baseman never had a chance. The ball hit the ground about twelve inches from his left heel and was by him before he could react. A delegation in the outfield ran to track it down.

The runner on third was on top of home plate in an instant and the runner on second was rounding third base as the third base coach swung his left arm like a windmill.

The little baseball park erupted into celebration. People went hog wild. There were people hugging and kissing each other. I noticed some people who were taking advantage of the situation.

Our coach was lying on his back between the pitcher's circle and second base. Players from our team were crawling all over him like a bunch of puppies. He was pushing them off to keep from being smothered.

Then that I spotted Joseph. He was wandering

around the infield with a confused look on his face. He approached an adult as though he were asking a question. He didn't get the answer he was looking for. He ran up to someone else. Suddenly, his faced brightened. He turned and spotted the celebration and ran and jumped in among his team mates. In a few minutes they were all in the back of a pickup truck. They sang "We're #1" all the way to the Sonic Drive-in.

That night when we returned home I had a burning question for our youngest. As I sat on the bed, he moved in close to me. I asked, "Joseph, this afternoon after the game, when everything was so crazy, I noticed you were wandering around the infield like you were lost. What was going on?"

He gave me a look that was serious but impatient and said emphatically, "I was trying to find out who won the game!"

And so I learned a great lesson about perspective. His and mine were a world apart that day. I celebrated the fact that there are still a few boys and girls who can participate in organized sports "just to be with my friends" and for the love of the game.

16

Gone Too Soon

Gone Too Soon

SHE WAS THE MOST POPULAR GIRL in the class of 1969 at Smith County High School. Her name was Cindy Gilbert. From a physical standpoint, Cindy had her slight imperfections. Her dazzling smile exposed teeth that were not perfectly straight and her nose was slightly hooked. That's not to say she was not attractive. On the contrary, she was a knock out. And her personality was off the charts. If I swore, I would have sworn that when God made Cindy Gilbert he put an extra swivel at the end of her backbone. Her personality even expressed itself in the way she walked. She was something else.

The thought of asking Cindy Gilbert for a date never even crossed my mind. By the time underclassmen guys had reached legal driving age, most of the popular girls were occupied with upperclassmen. But even more than that, if only on a subconscience level, I thought Cindy Gilbert was out of my league. Like I said, she was something else.

I loved Cindy Gilbert, not like a sister, and yet not like a girlfriend. I loved the person Cindy Gilbert. And we shared a unique connection.

During our underclassmen years, freshman, sophomore, and junior, when the members of our class elected Class Favorites, it was Cindy Gilbert every time. And in each of those years when the photographer took the Class Favorite photo for the high school annual, I was in the photo with Cindy every time. After our freshman year, just before the photographer snapped the picture, she would turn to me with that dazzling smile and say, "Well, here we are again." I will never forget the look on her face. I felt ten feet tall and bulletproof.

After high school, our lives took very different routes. I spent the next 15 years living my life. She spent those years fighting for hers.

Cindy Gilbert was the first person that I remember from our hometown of Carthage to make regular trips to the M.D. Anderson Cancer Center in Houston, Texas. For over 15 years, she endured chemotherapy and radiation treatments and was in and out of remission. Fortunately, she recovered for long enough periods of time to give birth to two beautiful children, a boy and a girl.

Living in different towns, we rarely saw each other over those years. I did manage to keep up with the state of her health through mutual friends.

In the spring of 1984, a few of our fellow class members pulled together an informal, 15-year reunion for the Class of 1969. I was glad to hear that Cindy was going to try to be there. Sure enough, she was. And rightfully, she was the center attention. I was thrilled when I got the chance to talk with her, one on one.

It was easy to see the years of treatment had taken a heavy toll. But those eyes of hers….oh, those eyes…..they were as sparkling and radiant as they were in our high school days. But they were different, too. They reflected a depth and wisdom and a peace that can only come from a long and difficult struggle in the center of life's crucible. She spoke easily about her life and her recent near death experiences.

"Jack, she said, "the first thing I noticed when I

started to die is that my perceptions just exploded. Everything became so much clearer. I experienced this heightened state of awareness that was simply indescribable." Her shining eyes grew brighter as she spoke of what she saw.

"The second time I 'died' I was in the presence of this incredible brightness," she continued. "And I could hear a conversation going on about me. One voice said, 'We've got to send her back.' I said, No, please let me go on." A voice countered, 'Just let her go on.' The other voice answered, 'We've got to send her back. There are too many praying for her.'"

Cindy gave me the look of a disappointed little girl; her mouth turned down at the corners, and she said, "So I had to come back."

Then she chirped, "But I told my doctors, the next time they lose me, just to let me go on." Then she smiled a tired smile and said, "Jack, I'm ready to go."

I knew she was.

Summer was hardly gone when I got the news that Cindy had indeed gone on.

Gone too soon....Cindy Gilbert was 33.

Over the years, I have often gone back for one reason or another to thumb through my old high school annuals. Ours was called The Owl. Oh, the crazy things that we wrote to one another in those days.

Check out this original line, "It has been fun going to school with you." Or this one, "Man, we will never forget that day in Biology class when...." Guess what? I forgot. And how about this little jewel, "Be good, be cool and don't do anything I would." Now that is strong advice.

A few years ago, I stumbled upon what Cindy wrote

to me in the 1967 Owl. Among the lines that she penned was this one, "You are a shining genius and you'll have an extra chance in life."

An extra chance.....I've given that a lot of thought since the day that I revisited that annual. An extra chance.....How could she have known? Or did she know? Was she a prophetess or just a teenage girl writing nice words?

An extra chance.....I suppose any of us who are still here have been given an extra chance. And each of us knows of someone who crossed the path of our lives and met an untimely death. They, too, were gone too soon. Maybe they were 10 or 18 or 21 or 33 or 47 or 69.... whatever their age.....gone too soon.

So what will we do with our extra chance? If we knew our days were numbered (by the way, they are) how would we live differently? If you knew you only had one more week, what would you do to make your last seven days count? What if you only had a month, or just one more year?

I would like to think that we would love more deeply. That we would work harder on the things that we consider most important. That we would breathe more deeply and be more aware of all that is going on around us. I think that we would place greater value on every fleeting moment. We would probably right some wrong we had done. And I'm sure that we would tell someone that we love them...... maybe for the first time.

An extra chance......you have been given one, you know.

John Wayne may have said it best in the movie, The Cowboys: "Boys [you too, girls] — we're burning daylight."

103

17

The
Lost Log Chain

The Lost Log Chain

MY FATHER WAS A MAN OF SIMPLE FAITH. That's not to say that he was a simple man.

Actually, he was quite complicated. But his faith was not complicated.

On the back side of our farm lies a five-acre field that we always called the potter field. It has been handed down through our family by word of mouth that the clay in the potter field was ideal for making Indian pottery. Whenever the potter field was plowed under, shards of pottery could be found in abundance. It was also easy to find arrow heads in the potter field. That led some of us to believe that an Indian village had once stood there.

I remember at least one tobacco patch situated in that field, but in later years the potter field went largely untended. The soil there may have been good for making pottery but it was also good for growing blackberry briars. My father saw to it that the potter field was bush-hogged at least once a year.

One fall it became necessary for my father to do some work in the potter field with his tractor and some equipment. He may have been cutting firewood and/or moving some downed trees. For whatever reason, while he was there, he misplaced his favorite log chain.

It is interesting to note that downed, mature blackberry briars are strikingly the same color of an old, well-used, rusty log chain. The potter field offered perfect camouflage for that which my father would later be searching.

My mother did not know about the lost log chain until my father began to "disappear" for an hour or two every morning and afternoon. Finally see quizzed him as to his whereabouts. He confided to her that he had lost his log chain and he had been slipping off to the potter field every day to look for it.

After a few days, news of my father's obsession with finding his lost log chain had circulated from family member to family member. On a Saturday morning, I stopped by the home place to check in on things.

I went in the house to visit with my mother first, as was my usual custom. We had only visited a minute when she asked if I had heard about the log chain. I assured her that I had. She said, "Well, he found it." Her face took on the excitement of a little girl as she continued, "But I'll let him tell you about it." I had a feeling that something special was in the wind.

I headed out toward the barn where my father was usually found. When he saw me coming across the yard, he came out to meet me. He smiled his patented shy smile and said, "Hello, Jackson B." He always greeted me that way in his later years.

And then, as if he were a little boy who could hardly wait to tell a secret, he asked, "Did you hear about my log chain?"

I said, "Well, I heard you lost it."

He beamed a smile as he said, "I found it yesterday just before dark." Then he settled back and, in a reflective voice, began his story. "Jack I lost that log chain over a week ago. I started looking for it on Monday morning, and

I looked for it every morning and every afternoon for a week."

"I'll bet you I covered that entire potter field twenty or thirty times," he continued.

"I would start at the edge of the field on one side and walk all the way across and then move over a few feet and head back to the other side. Then I would crisscross the field the same way. I covered every inch of it."

In my mind's eye I could see him crossing the field — his back bent forward, his hands joined behind his back, his eyes glued to the ground in front of him.

Then, his voice took on a somber tone. "Late Friday afternoon, I had just about given up. I had been looking for an hour or two and the sun had gone down.

It was just beginning to get dark when I headed back toward the house."

"When I got to the middle of the potter field, I decided I would stop and pray. I bowed my head and closed my eyes, and I said, 'Lord, you know I've lost my log chain. And you know I've been looking for it for a week. I've done everything I know to do and I can't find it. Will you please help me find my log chain?'"

"Jack," he said, "When I opened my eyes, I was looking it. The chain was curled up about three feet in front of my right foot."

His eyes were filled with tears and a childlike wonder. And in those sparkling eyes I could see joy and gratitude and a "knowing." And I "knew," too, that my father had experienced an encounter with the God of the universe over a lost log chain.

G. Campbell Morgan, a great English preacher of two centuries ago, was once asked by a woman, "Brother

Morgan, do you think we should concern God with little matters?" His answer was this: "Madam, what is there with our great God that is not a little matter?"

18

Giving Up The Car Keys

Giving up the Car Keys

THE BABY BOOMERS HAVE BEEN REFERRED to as the "sandwich generation" because, quite simply, we found ourselves "between." As sandwich filling is placed between two pieces of bread, our generation found itself between two very different generations of people, each posing unique dilemmas for us.

Whereas our generation was defined by the word "expectation," our Generation X, Next, and Y children's generations can be defined by the word "entitlement." They matured later, stayed at home longer, and after leaving the nest, many came back home to roost again. That gave some members of their generation another name, "the boomerang kids."

We baby boomers face serious issues regarding our World War II generation parents that other generations have not faced. Among them are a myriad of healthcare issues, long term care decisions, and yes, even timing issues with car keys. Many tough decisions must be made. Most are issues of the heart. The emotional toll can become overwhelming.

When my father's physical and mental health began to decline, his driving became a subject of heightened discussion among family members. By then, his travels had become limited to Sunday church, a trip two miles west down Highway 70, and regular errands to Carthage, three miles east on the same familiar highway. He liked to drive

to town at least two times a week to purchase gas at his
favorite market. He reasoned that it was important to keep
the gas tank as full as possible. His trips to buy gas took
him through a three-way stop at the end of the Cordell
Hull Bridge and straight into South Carthage.

Then came the day when, on one of his trips, my
father found himself in downtown Carthage, disoriented
and confused as to where he was. He finally wandered
down to the Smith County Jail, walked inside, and
consulted the receptionist as to his location. Fortunately,
she knew him. With the assistance of a deputy, they
helped my father find his car and showed him how to get
out of town. When he returned home my mother noticed
that he was visibly upset because he had gotten lost.

After that day, at her own personal risk, my mother
decided to accompany him whenever he ran his errands.
The first few trips went fine. Then one day when my
father brought the car to a stop at the end of the Cordell
Hull Bridge, he turned to my mother, and asked, "Which
way do we go now?" She would later recall, "That's the
day I knew we were in trouble."

Over the next weeks my mother began to suggest to
my father that it might not be in his best interest to
continue driving. Her approach was nothing short of
masterful. She reasoned that it was not his driving that
worried her. It was all those "young folks."

She told him, "Daddy, these 'young folks' are just too
fast for us. I'm afraid we're not quick enough to get out of
their way." He didn't argue the point.

Eventually, after some family discussion, my brother
John, who worked on the family farm, began to drive my
father's car to his house at day's end. He would return it

the next morning. As time passed we began to refer to my father's car as "John's car."

The strategy was subtle but effective. My father seemed to accept it.

In the following days, John would show up each Sunday morning just in time to drive my father to church. Errands to town were soon forgotten. Unfortunately, the issue of my father's driving had not been completely put to bed.

Outside of those trips to town and church on Sunday, my mother and father didn't travel very much in their later years. They did make three annual trips outside Smith County. On Mother's Day they visited my brother Tom's house in Lafayette, and on the Fourth of July, my brother Dewey's house in Hillsdale, Tennessee; they spent Thanksgiving Day at my family's house in Hartsville. Even when my father was still driving them, he had a little familiar routine that he would initiate after the noon meal. About mid-afternoon, he would start sending this message to my mother, "Ma, are you 'bout ready to go home?" It was always the same. He would get more and more restless as the day wore on. Finally, my mother would relent and they would head home, always well before dark.

He made his last family get-together away from home on July 4, 2002, a little less that a year before he died. That morning John stopped by the home place and picked up my mother and father. On the way out to the car my father announced that he thought he might drive. Upon my mother's insistence and with John's cooperation, they managed to convince him to ride in the passenger seat. He reluctantly complied.

We should have seen it coming.

They arrived in Hillsdale that day to great fanfare. At this point in their lives my mother was using two walking canes and my father was using one. I called them the "three-cane brigade." They made it into the house, got all settled in and we all enjoyed a great lunch. My father, however, seemed a bit unsettled and inquired continuously as to Ma's whereabouts. And, right after lunch he started asking, "Is Ma 'bout ready to go home?" He asked everybody, over and over again. I sent word to John, "Dad is unusually restless. Keep an eye on him. Don't let him beat you to the car."

The afternoon got away from us. The next thing I knew, one of the grandchildren in a breathless voice was exclaiming, "Uncle Jack, come quick. Pa is in the car, behind the wheel and won't get out. Aunt Sissy said to hurry!" A thousand thoughts raced through my head as I bolted outside. None of them were very pleasant.

When I arrived outside, sure enough, there he was. He was in the driver's seat, behind the wheel, hunkered down. I could tell by his body language that wild horses were not going to pull him out of that car. My sister was already trying to talk him out of the car. It appeared that the discussion had been going on for few minutes.

In a loud voice that appeared to be irritating him, she said, "Now, Daddy, you need to let John drive."

"Why?" he snapped, "I can drive just fine."

"I know that you can drive, but it would be better if you let John drive today,"she reasoned.

"There is nothing wrong with my driving," he pressed.

"Oh, I know that, Daddy," she said. "But it's just better if John drives."

"I know what you're trying to say," he snarled, "You're saying I can't drive!"(To him, she was saying that he was not capable of driving.)

"Oh, I'm not saying that, Daddy!" she responded. (Yes, she was.)

My brother Dewey is a mild-mannered guy. He had quietly observed my sister's futile efforts. He stepped up and softly said, "Now, Daddy, it's probably better if you let John drive."

My father turned to Dewey, cocked one eye and announced his decision, "I'm driving this car home."

I motioned with my hand for Dewey and Shari to step my way. I whispered, "We'd better let Mother handle this." I turned toward the house. She had just stepped outside and onto the deck.

I moved quickly. When I reached her side, I whispered, "Mother, we have a little problem."

"What's your problem?" she asked.

I said, "Well, Dad's in the drivers seat, and says he is driving the car home."

She paused for a moment as if she were gathering her wits, then in a serious voice, she declared softly, "I'll handle this."

I stepped back out of her way.

When she arrived at the car I noticed that the window was down on the passenger side. She slowly handed her canes to me. Then, she clamped her hands down on the top of the door. She leaned into the window, looked straight into my father's eyes and in a calm but stern voice, she said, "Alright, buddy, you've got two choices."

I noticed immediately that she limited his options.

She nodded toward the passenger seat, and pointing in the same direction with the index finger of her right hand, she said, "You can ride here." Then her words slowed as she gave a hitchhiker's thumb with her left hand toward the back seat as she said, "Or you can ride in the back." She paused slightly before she continued, "Which is it going to be?"

I further noticed that of the two options she offered him, driving the car was not one of them.

My father's eyes narrowed with rage. And for a moment he looked from side to side like a wild animal that had been cornered. Then he caught himself, and in a voice that could not conceal his anger, he barked, "I'll tell you where I'm going to ride!" Pointing at the passenger seat, he declared, "I'm going to sit right there where I can see what's going on!"

It was the only consolation and pride that he could salvage. At least he could be up front and keep John from messing up.

He opened his door and struggled to get out of the car. Then he held on with his right hand as he limped around the car. He seemed as embarrassed as he was furious. The man in me wept silently for this, my father, who had always been so strong and so sure of himself. And now, to beat it all, his bluff had been called right out in front of God and everybody.

He climbed in the car and took his seat. He closed his door firmly, without slamming it. He was seething.

I whispered in my mother's ear, "Mother, he's as mad as a cat."

She said, "I know it."

Then I said, "Here's what I want you to try. When

117

you get started up the road, lay your left hand on his left shoulder and squeeze it softly. Then leave your hand on his shoulder and see what happens."

She grinned and whispered, "Okay."

John slid behind the wheel, started the engine, and they slowly drove away. I was worried for my Dad.

Early in the evening, well before their bedtime, I called my mother just to make sure they'd arrived home safely and gotten into the house alright. But I had another reason for calling. I was concerned about my father's state of mind.

When my mother answered the phone, I was surprised by the energy in her voice.

I asked, "Mother, did y'all make it home okay?"

"Oh, yes," she chirped. "We made it just fine! Didn't we have a wonderful day?"

"Yes, we surely did," I agreed. "How is Dad?"

"Oh, he's just fine," she purred. Then she paused.

"Jack, it was the funniest thing," she said. "After we left Dewey's house and got started up the road, I placed my left hand on Daddy's shoulder and I squeezed it softly."

I smiled to myself, but I was a little shocked because she was sounding like it was her idea.

"Well," she said, "for a minute or two nothing happened. Then, he laid his right hand on top of my hand and patted it tenderly. Then, he left his hand on top of mine."

She sounded like a school girl as she giggled softly, "We held hands all the way home!"

I love happy tears. I couldn't hold them back. I didn't let her know.

They were married for over sixty years. When you've

been together that long, a simple touch can communicate so very many things. My sister-in-law Patsy has always observed that Ma and Pa were always "touchin' and pattin'."

That afternoon when my mother laid her hand on Daddy's shoulder and squeezed it she was saying, "I'm sorry I had to talk so straight to you and I know I've made you mad, but it's just best that you not drive. But I love you, and you're my horse if you don't ever win another race!"

And by responding with his hand and holding hers, he was saying, "Yes, I'm mad. You hurt my feeling. And, I know I don't need to be driving. But it's hard to give up things that I have always done. I love you, too."

Sadly, the generations who have succeeded those of the World War II era have failed to understand the depth of living that can only be achieved by remaining committed and faithful over many years.

19

The
Power of
Words

The Power of Words

MY FATHER WAS A MEMBER OF THAT GROUP to whom news anchor Tom Brokaw referred as the Greatest Generation. A veteran of World War II, he served in the US Army Air Corp in the European theater. His specialty was the C-47 cargo plane, the forerunner to the first commercial airliner, the DC-3.

Like most of his fellow veterans, he rarely talked about his war experiences. He sometimes would tell of how he was "weathered in" in Paris, France, for a period of six weeks one spring, and how on most mornings he and his buddies would stroll down to the Eiffel Tower. I think those were the most carefree moments that he experienced during the war.

He never told us of how his pilot, his best friend, died. My mother shared that story with each of us children.

It seems that his pilot came to him one morning and suggested that they take a long walk out in the French countryside. For reasons known only to him, my father declined the offer, saying he would rather stay in town that day. While taking his walk, my father's best war buddy stepped on a landmine. He would never return. We never knew his buddy's name. I guess it was a story too painful to tell.

But there was one war story that my father loved to tell. Toward the end of his life, he told it often. Some days he would tell it more than once. His telling that story became a priceless treasure to his children. We could never hear it often enough.

My father would ask, "Did I ever tell you the story about the British general?" Whether it was one of my brothers or my sister or me, we would always answer, "No, Dad, I don't believe you did." That was our answer even if he had told it just yesterday.

He would smile the most pleasurable smile and then settle into his story by saying, "Well, you know, when I was in the war I worked on the old C-47 airplane. The engines on that particular plane were bad about leaking oil. When a gasket went bad that engine would sling oil everywhere.

"There was a British general who was grounded in Paris where I was stationed because one of the engines on his C-47 engine was losing too much oil. And he was desperate to get back to England. One day he was telling a young American GI about his dilemma. The GI told him, 'I know a boy from Tennessee who can fix your plane,' and the general replied, 'Go get him.'"

The general asked my father to take a look at the plane and then asked if he could repair it. My father told him that, yes, he could perform the necessary repairs but that he would need some parts.

The general said, "You tell me what you need and I'll have the parts here by this afternoon." The parts arrived as promised and my father worked into the night to repair the engine.

The next morning my father, his navigator and the pilot took the plane up for a test run. When they landed, my father left to get some sleep.

Later in the day the British general returned to find his plane airworthy. His words to the American GI were these, "They should make an officer out of that boy from

Tennessee."

When my father told that part of the story, he would laugh a laugh that was uniquely his own. And then, his eyes sparkling, he would say, "That was sump 'un, wasn't it?"

I have come to believe that he considered it one of his finest moments… a moment made possible by the British general's words of praise…..words he remembered for a lifetime.

Almost twenty years ago, my mother called to inform me that my photograph, along with a write-up, was on the front page of the local newspaper, the Carthage Courier. She seemed excited about the fact that I would be speaking to the local Farm Bureau on the coming Saturday night and mildly irritated that I had not "said anything about it."

I explained that I had not considered it that big of a deal. She admitted that she and my father "didn't get out much anymore, especially at night."

But then, she said, "Your father is talking like he might come to the meeting."

I didn't get my hopes up, but when I arrived at the Smith County High School cafeteria that evening, there he was. He had come to hear his boy make a talk.

Well, I made the talk and the audience members seemed to have a great time. We laughed together over my stories of growing up on the farm.

When the evening was over, I visited with old friends and shared parting words. All the while, I noticed that my father lingered.

When everyone was gone, I sat down with my father for a few rare moments of quiet conversation.

In recent years I had been giving serious

consideration to a career as a professional speaker. I had observed some of the greatest platform speakers of our time, including Zig Ziglar, Dr. Ken McFarland, Ira Hayes, and Cavett Robert, to mention a few. And on this evening, I thought it an opportune time to run the idea by my father. So I launched into my explanation.

I said, "Dad if you get good enough at telling your stories, and if you do it long enough to become the best, eventually you can make a living inspiring people and making them laugh. Clients pay all your travel expenses. It's a great way......"

I stopped in mid-sentence. As I peered into his sky-blue eyes, I could tell that he was not following me. Then, I realized that the only speakers that my father had ever heard were military training officers in World War II and country Baptist preachers. The concept of a motivational humorist was not in his quiver of arrows!

"Dad, do you understand what I'm saying?" I asked.

I will never forget his words.

"Naw, son," he softly admitted. "I can't say that I do. But I'll tell you one thing. No matter what you try, I'm for you."

His words will do me until the day that I die.

I think that William Barclay may have said it best:

"One of the highest of human duties is the duty of encouragement.

It is easy to laugh at men's ideas; it is easy to pour cold water on their enthusiasm; it is easy to discourage others. The world is filled with discouragers. We have a Christian duty to encourage one another. Many a time a word of praise or thanks or appreciation or cheer has kept a man on his feet. Blessed is the man who speaks such a word."

20

The
Long
Goodbye

The Long Goodbye

I AM ONE OF THOSE FORTUNATE sons who can say my father was the best man I have ever known. He was a prince of a man. He was patient and kind and, in every sense, a man of his word. He was respectful to our mother and in all the years that I knew him he never once made an off-color comment. If a scene came on TV that he thought was too risqué, he turned it off and no one watched. He was a quiet man, not a conversationalist, but his life spoke volumes. He spent seventy-nine of his eighty-one years showing us how to live. He spent the last two showing us how to die.

Soon after he was no longer able to operate his farm equipment, his physical and mental capabilities began to deteriorate noticeably. At first he had difficulty with his sense of balance. Then he began to experience dementia. For over a year his doctor insisted that he did not have Alzheimer's disease. But eventually his symptoms became overwhelming. Before he died he was a classic case. And in those days that he experienced both dementia and Alzheimer's disease, our father did and said some of the funniest things.

I am fortunate, too, in that my family has always enjoyed the many benefits of a healthy sense of humor. It is a bittersweet time when someone you love begins to slip away from you. But when my father said and did funny things, we laughed. We laughed a lot.

My father was a good-looking man. And he knew it. And he liked to be complimented, especially in his later years. Almost up until the day he died, he liked to be clean-shaven and he liked for his hair to be neatly cut and combed. Even after he became bed-ridden he would sit up in bed, propped up by pillows, with a kingly countenance on his face.

One day my brother Tom stopped by to see my father. During his visit he said, "Dad, you look real good today."

My father answered, "You know, I've looked that way all day today."

On another occasion when my father was more deeply into Alzheimer's, my brother Dewey was spending time with him and in the course of the conversation Dewey asked, "Do you have any children?"

My father said, "Oh, yes, I have four boys and a girl." Then he quickly rattled off their names, "Tom, Jack, John, and Dewey, and the girl's name is Shari." Dewey pointed to a large photograph of the four sons that hung above the mantle and asked, "Are those your boys?"

My father beamed, "That's them." Dewey pointed to Tom and asked, "Who is this?" My father said, "That's Tom." Dewey pointed to me. My father said, "That's Jack." Dewey pointed to John. My father said, "That's John." Dewey pointed to himself in the photo and asked, "Who's this?" My father studied for a moment and then said,

"I don't know who he is. You'll have to ask one of the other boys."

In the last few months before he became bed-ridden, my father developed a habit of sleeping with his clothes on — I mean, fully dressed. Along with his long underwear, he wore his shirt and pants, his shoes, his red and black plaid wool cap, and even a light jacket. That wool cap provided a special memory for me.

Whenever I said my goodbyes after visiting my parents, I initiated a little ritual that I would go through with my father. First, I would say, "I love you, Dad."

He would answer, "I love you, too, son."

Then, I would say, "You're a 'good 'un."

He would repeat, "You're a 'good 'un, too."

Then I would lean over and kiss him on his forehead. Those kisses always tasted of salt. That hot cap made for a sweaty head. It is a taste I will long remember.

In my father's bedroom on the wall to his left as he lay on the bed hung two photographs. One was Frank III, my brother Tom's son, the first grandchild. The other was a photograph of my sister Shari. Both were pictures of bright-eyed toddlers with glowing smiles. For some reason and for a span of time that lasted several weeks, my father began to refer to them as 'Jack's boys.' Of course, he had not completely missed the mark. I do have three boys. That just wasn't them on the wall.

He took delight in shining a flashlight on the photographs to "make them laugh." Whenever someone entered his bedroom, my father would often ask, his eyes glowing, "Have you seen 'Jack's boys'?" Whether we answered yes or no, he would say, "Watch this." Then, he would point his flashlight in their direction. When the beam of the flashlight shone on their bright faces, he would chuckle and say, "Watch 'em laugh! They really like it when I shine this light on them."

Eventually, everyone in the family had heard about or had been introduced to "Jack's boys." Most had participated in the flashlight routine at least once. My father insisted that "'Jack's boys' laugh every time I shine this light on them." It became a special little joy to him to show off "Jack's boys laughing."

As my father's mental capacities continued to slip, he also experienced less than desirable control of certain physical functions, particularly his kidneys, and especially at night.

One morning when my mother walked into his bedroom to check on him, she found him sitting on the side of the bed. He was holding his arms out from his sides and he was looking down at his front. She said he was wet from just below his chin all the way down to his knees, and the look on his face was one of absolute disbelief. With surprise in her voice, she exclaimed, "What in the world has happened to you?"

He turned his gaze toward her and with a tone of amused aggravation, he said, "One of 'Jack's boys' has peed all over me!"

A little more than a year before my father died, I visited him and my mother on a cold winter's day. My brothers, my sister and I were checking in on them even more than usual because my mother had fallen the week before and was temporarily confined to her bed. As I rang the doorbell that morning I knew my father was my only hope to unlock the front door. I rang the door bell a second time and waited. In my mind's eye I could see him lying on top of his bedcovers, fully dressed from his shoes to his red and black plaid wool cap. I rang the doorbell a third time and waited.

Finally, I saw his shadow drifting into the kitchen. Then he appeared in the doorway, silver cane in hand. He was carefully checking things out. He turned slowly to his left and surveyed the kitchen. Then he turned slowly to his right and peered down the hall in my direction. He proceeded cautiously down the hall, looking from side to side as if everything were new to him. He checked out the living room thoroughly as he made his way to the front door. When he saw me through the glass in the front door, he smiled and raised his hand and waved. I returned his wave. Then I leaned up close to the door and in a loud voice I said, "Dad, open the door." He seemed to think this was a good idea. He smiled and said, "Okay." He transferred his cane to his left hand and jiggled the doorknob with his right hand. With a perplexed look on his face, he looked back at me and he said, "Won't open." Again, in a loud voice, I said, "Go get a key from Ma." He thought that was a good idea, too. His face brightened and he said, "Okay!" He left me and was gone for what seemed like a half day.

Finally, I saw his shadow creeping into the kitchen again and I knew he was making a return trip. He was every bit as cautious as before. Slowly but surely, he made his way to the front door again. When he arrived at the front door he smiled and waved just as before. I leaned into the door and gave the instructions again, "Dad, open the door." He smiled and said, "Okay." He gave the doorknob a twist or two, looked perplexed again, and said, "Won't open." I answered back, "Go get a key from Ma!" He smiled and said, "Okay!"

Then he threw me a curve. Instead of going back toward the bedroom, he turned and stepped slowly over to his favorite chair. He held on to it carefully until he could slowly collapse into its seat. Then he slipped off his shoes, took off his cap and laid it aside and started rocking. I had been forgotten.

But I didn't give up easily. I walked around to the back of the house to my mother's bedroom window. I pecked on the window. She immediately recognized my voice. After hearing of my dilemma, she insisted on slipping a key to me through the storm window. That was quite an undertaking. Finally the key found its way through a tiny slot in the edge of the window. She smiled. I took the key and headed back around the house.

I unlocked the front door and stepped inside. I spoke to my dad. He seemed happy to see me. Then I went back to the bedroom to see my mother. My curiosity had gotten the best of me. I had a burning question to ask my mother. After we had chatted for a moment or two, I asked my question, "Mother, what did he say to you when he first came back here to get the door key?"

She said, "Well, I asked him, 'who's at the front door?'" And he said, 'I don't know him, but he's been here before!'"

President Ronald Reagan referred to Alzheimer's disease as "The Long Goodbye." And so it was with our family. Our father began to leave us long before he was gone.

In the days of his long goodbye, we were afforded time to cherish his life in ways that would have been missed had he gone suddenly. And from the time his health began to fail until the day he died, he faced his declining health and death with a calmness and serenity that was nothing short of saintly.

He talked with God often, and in those moments his wholeness seemed to return.

It became evident that over the course of his life he

and God had become good friends.

Our father showed us a good death.

On the day before he died, I paid him and my mother a visit. When it came time for me to leave I sat on the side of his bed to do my familiar routine.

When I said, "I love you, Dad", he smiled a tired smile but did not respond.

I said, "You're a good 'un." He slowly looked away. I kissed his forehead that tasted of salt, not knowing it would be the last time.

In the early hours of the next morning he quietly slipped away and finished his good bye.